CO-OPPORTUNITY

THE RISE OF A COMMUNITY OWNED MARKET

BY DAVID J. THOMPSON
A Personal Recollection

Foreword by Ann M. Evans
Welcome by Dean Kubani
Afterword by Bruce Palma

Twin Pines Press
Davis, California

Book design by Blackstone Edge, with thanks to Donna Pizzi for her editing, layout and design skills, and to Marshal Serna, for Technical Direction

Cover design by Alan Munoz, Graphics Coordinator, Co-opportunity
Thanks to Bruce Palma, Audrey Beim & Latoya Woods at Co-opportunity for their generous help with the completion of this book

DEDICATIONS

This book about Co-opportunity is dedicated first to my family for supporting my decades of commitment not just to Co-opportunity but also to cooperatives in the USA and throughout the world.

Thanks in particular to my wonderful wife, Ann M. Evans, our daughter, Hatley Rose Evans Thompson, to my brother Philip Clayton-Thompson, my sister-in-law, Donna Pizzi, my mother-in-law, Audrey Lippman, and my niece, Rayne Thompson, and her two boys, Finn Philip and Reed David. Each one of you has given me such love, help and guidance. Each one of you has dedicated part of your lives also to cooperatives. Rayne is the sixth generation of Thompsons to work for a cooperative.

It is also dedicated to those friends in the cooperative movement who helped me build Co-opportunity in particular and cooperatives everywhere and share my yearning to build a better world. Thank you.

Next, to the many board members, staff and members of Co-opportunity, Associated Cooperatives, the Davis Food Co-op, and the Twin Pines Cooperative Foundation, who I have served with and gained from during over three decades of service to cooperatives.

And lastly, to the present Board of Co-opportunity for supporting the book, to Will Simon for saving the store, and Bruce Palma for helping Co-opportunity to not just survive but thrive.

PRINTED IN THE USA

TABLE OF CONTENTS

Greetings from Kevin Mc Keown, Mayor of Santa Monica..........................*viii*
Welcome by Dean Kubani, Board President of Co-opportunity....................*xi*
Accolades from Co-opportunity Board Members Past and Present...........*xv*
Foreword by Ann M. Evans, former Mayor of Davis....................................*xxi*
Introduction by Author...*xxvii*

1 A Story of Starting Co-opportunity: the Beginning Years...........................1
2 California Co-ops, the Depression, World War II and Beyond....................5
3 The Critical Role of the Santa Monica Co-op..13
4 The Santa Monica Co-op Group that Formed Co-opportunity................19
5 Direct Charge Co-ops Appear in Canada & Come to California.............25
6 How did Co-opportunity gets its Name?...31
7 The Old Santa Monica Co-op Dies as We are Being Born.......................35
8 Finding Broadway..39

    Photos
    A. Co-opportunity's West Los Angeles Beginnings
    B. The First Santa Monica Co-op Store
    C. Co-op Background – History, People & Today's Store

9 Co-opportunity Opens on Broadway...61
10 Cracks Appear in Our Co-op..65
11 Where Does Money Come From?..71
12 Building Community, Cooperatives and the Santa Monica
    Farmers Market..75
13 You're Kidding! You People Want a Loan?...85
14 Helping Start the Venice Ocean Park Co-operative Commonwealth....91
15 Concluding the Beginning Years...95
16 Afterword and the Future by Bruce Palma, General Manager,
    Co-opportunity..99
17 120 More Food Co-ops on the Way, Stuart Reid, E.D. Food
    Co-op Initiative (FCI)..117
18 Accolades from Co-op Leaders Across America......................................121
19 LET'S WIN THE $10,000 MATCHING GRANT!..................................129
Congratulatory Messages to Co-opportunity..134
Author's Bio...137

ACCOLADES TO CO-OPPORTUNITY

The Author wishes to thank the following people for providing us with the accolades, greetings and commendations that are found within this book about Co-opportunity.

Terry Appleby, *Past Chair, National Cooperative Grocers and GM Hanover Co-op*

Patricia Cumbie, *Author, Growing with Purpose: Forty Years of Seward Community Cooperative*

Sahaja Douglass, *Board Member, Co-opportunity*

Ann M. Evans, *Former Mayor of Davis & Co-Founder Davis Food Co-op and Davis Farmers Market, Former Cooperative Development Director, State of California*

Ruth Goldway, *Former Board Member Co-opportunity, former Mayor of Santa Monica*

Dave Gutknecht, *Editor, Cooperative Grocer*

Ann Hoyt, *Cooperative Hall of Fame Inductee 2015, former Chair, National Cooperative Business Association, CCMA Superstar*

Michelle Jacobson, *Board Member, Co-opportunity and former board member Twin Pines Cooperative Foundation, Trustee Howard Bowers Fund*

Richard Katz, *former Democratic Leader, California Assembly*

Jens Koepke, *Board Member, Co-opportunity and Board Member Twin Pines Cooperative Foundation*

Dean Kubani, *President, Co-opportunity and Board Member Twin Pines Cooperative Foundation*

Frances Moore Lappé, *Author, "Diet for a Small Planet," and forty other books*

David Lippman, *Past General Manager, North Coast Cooperatives and Board Member, Twin Pines Cooperative Foundation*

Stephanie Mandel, *Marketing Manager, Briarpatch Co-op*

Dan Nordley, *Publisher, Cooperative Grocer & Past CEO, Cooperative Information Network*

Bruce Palma, *General Manager, Co-opportunity*

Stuart Reid, *Executive Director, Food Co-op Initiative*

Derek Shearer, *Ambassador, Chevalier Professor of Diplomacy, Occidental College*

Robynn Shrader, *CEO, National Cooperative Grocers*

Karen Zimbelman, *Director of Cooperative and Member Relations, National Cooperative Grocers*

Kevin McKeown
Mayor

City Council
1685 Main Street, Room 209
Santa Monica
CA 90401

City of
Santa Monica®

July 23, 2015

Only one Santa Monica membership card in my wallet is older and more worn
than my Co-opportunity card, and that one is from the Santa Monica Public Library.
Co-opportunity has been part of my life since I moved here almost forty years ago,
a vegetarian hungry for affordable options.

The underlying concepts of Co-opportunity were hardly foreign to me. The New
Haven Rochdale commune, which I visited often, was just five blocks up Elm Street
from the campus radio station where I spent most of my time at Yale in the late
sixties. I might have thought we were uniquely the "cooperation generation," but
learned that the Rochdale principles dated to the 1840s – and are alive into the 21st
century through community institutions like Co-opportunity.

David Thompson, in "Co-opportunity — a Westside Story," describes how those
defining principles of cooperation inspired Santa Monicans forty years ago to create
what is now the largest and oldest retail food cooperative in Los Angeles County.

As you'll read in this history, Co-opportunity's genesis was deeply intertwined with
local grassroots activism that led to Santa Monicans for Renters' Rights, and a four-
decade run of progressive politics in Santa Monica. Co-opportunity and our farmers'
markets challenged the corporatization of not only food but of our society.

The Co-opportunity Board is not suited shadows in some distant skyscraper. It's the
long-time leader of our City government's Office of Sustainability and the
Environment; the mother of a Samohi student who convinced me to fund her trip to
the World Social Forum, and who became the youngest state legislator in Vermont
history; the owner and former publisher of our local daily newspaper.

As Mayor of Santa Monica, and a Co-opportunity member/owner, I congratulate us,
every one, on forty years of principled, productive, partnership. We do best for
ourselves when we do best for each other.

Kevin McKeown

CO-OPPORTUNITY 41ST ANNIVERSARY

Our door at
11556 Santa Monica Blvd, West Los Angeles
first opened on August 24, 1974

Our doors at 1530 Broadway in Santa Monica
first opened on July 5, 1976

Our doors at 1525 Broadway, Santa Monica
first opened on December 1, 1995

BOARD OF DIRECTORS 2015

Dean Kubani, *President*
Jens Koepke, *Vice-President*
Ross Furukawa, *Treasurer*
Michelle Jacobson, *Secretary*
Steve Bornstein
Lynn Dickinson
Sahaja Douglass
Bernie Estefan
Carl Fredlin
Ross Kurakawa

General Manager
Bruce Palma

General Manager Emeritus
Will Simon

WWW.COOPPORTUNITY.COM

WELCOME

From Dean Kubani, *Board President, Co-opportunity*

If you are a member of Co-opportunity, you are probably aware of what a unique and special place it is. However, if you don't know much about Co-opportunity, when you will read this book, you will learn many of the reasons for that specialness (and, hopefully, will become a member yourself!).

Why have so many people come to Co-opportunity and become loyal members? And why did a small but growing group of committed people work so hard for so many years to create Co-opportunity and volunteer their time to help keep it going? The answer to those questions goes far beyond the natural foods that Co-opportunity sells.

Yes, it is true that Co-opportunity was started primarily to address the dearth in the availability wholesome, natural and organic foods in the early 1970s. But Co-opportunity never was nor is just a natural foods store. What set it apart from other grocery stores when it opened in 1974, and even more so now, are the ideals upon which the store was founded.

Co-opportunity's specialness derives from the fact that it is part of a large and transformative movement. Our history can be traced from 1974, back to the opening of the original Santa Monica Consumers Cooperative Society store in 1935, and then all the way back to the 1840s, in England, where the co-operative movement was first started. That movement now involves thousands of co-operative enterprises throughout the world and has created an alternative economic model, where people and the planet matter more than profit. I don't know about you but the fact that this movement exists, and is thriving, gives me a great amount of hope for the future.

While for-profit companies and corporations are first and foremost (and often entirely) focused on making money, Co-opportunity, and co-ops in general, are all about people, and making people's lives better, and creating communities and economies that support people. The profits from our store go back to our members, and enable us to provide living wages and benefits to our employees. They support local charities, schools and events and even help new co-ops get started in other communities.

I think David Thompson sums up the reasons for Co-opportunity's specialness and uniqueness perfectly in his introduction to this history: "We are a self-made enterprise and self-capitalized by our members in an era when we are led to believe that ordinary people cannot and should not enter business together. We do not act to gain profit by our investment but that our investment would fund our shared goals about food and community. We seek a better world."

When you shop in the store, when you become a member, and when you get involved in the Co-opportunity community, you become a part of that movement that is making our community and the world a better place. I hope you enjoy this history of a remarkable store, and then come in and see, perhaps with a slightly new perspective, how special a place it has become. And I also invite you to then start looking to the future and dreaming about what is next.

ACCOLADES FROM CO-OPPORTUNITY BOARD MEMBERS
(FORMER AND PRESENT)

Throughout the twenty years I have shopped at the Co-op, I have seen it transform from a small, somewhat dusty market into a beautiful, vibrant store offering 100% organic produce, high quality consciously raised meat, poultry and dairy, and a large selection of other products that support our health. In spite of all the wonderful and nourishing items sold, what draws me to the Co-op is the warm, caring group of employees and shoppers. It is not like any other store in town; at the Co-op people know me and my family. We care about each other and I have not experienced that sense of community in any other place I shop.

Sahaja Douglass, Member of Co-opportunity Board of Directors, 2009-present

David Thompson brought me into Co-opportunity in the early 1970s. He showed me the connection between my advocacy for better regulation of food safety, labeling and access and the practical, hands-on solutions being developed by Santa Monica volunteers in my own backyard. I am very proud that I was on the board and part of the early years of Co-opportunity, and I recognize how the store helped me in my later efforts to build farmers markets in Santa Monica when I was that city's mayor. Co-opportunity is now an established, well-respected retail leader. Thank you, David, for writing this history of how remarkably successful people can be when working together for the common good.

Ruth Goldway, Former Co-opportunity Board Member and former Mayor of Santa Monica

I joined the Board of Co-opportunity in 1989. It was a transitional time from a grassroots, make-it-up-as-we-go store to the professionally managed, thriving enterprise we are today. If you take our current success for granted, David Thompson's chronicle of Co-opportunity's early years is a must-read. This is an inspirational memoir of a tremendously dedicated, visionary group of pioneers who realized a transformation and revolution in the retail food industry. Today, Co-opportunity is among the largest, most successful coops in the country. In Santa Monica, we have a thriving farmers market, organic food is available in every traditional grocery store and consumers are making healthier choices. But this revolution is not over. Co-opportunity and its members can continue to lead the movement for GMO labeling, food security and ensuring that concern for people is a value of those in the food industry.

Thank you, David, for nurturing Co-opportunity through its early years, writing this book and inspiring me to work for our cooperative future.

Michelle Jacobson, Co-opportunity Board Member (1989 – Present) Past President (2002-2004), Past Twin Pines Cooperative Foundation Board Member and Howard Bowers Fund Trustee

---

I have been a Co-opportunity member for over 25 years and a member of the Board of Directors for 21 years. I joined the Co-op because my 6 year-old-son, at the time, was having sever asthma attacks, usually at midnight, often resulting in a rushed trip to the hospital for an adrenalin shot. After the third hospital visit, I was warned by the doctor at St. John's to do something different because the asthma would only get worse, and if the adrenalin didn't work, my son could die.

A week later, a co-worker gave me the book, "Recalled by Life," and I became macrobiotic. My macrobiotic teacher made me shop at the Co-op. This was the old building across the street from where we are now. I was in the bulk section looking for aduki beans. I couldn't find them and asked this grey bearded man for help. He told me, "We" call them azuki beans. He helped me with the rest of my shopping list.

This gentleman was none other than Eytan Ben Sheviya, one of the original founders of the Co-op. Since then, every time I see someone with a list, I help them in my Co-op way. After this I became involved with Co-opportunity and joined the Board of Directors.

Emil K. Kalil, Ph.D. Former Board Member.

The View Forward And Back – Co-opportunity At 40

I have been on the Board of Co-opportunity since the late 90s, and I would define that period as one of solidifying professional management, more efficient Board governance and national integration.

Having become over the years deeply reliant on Will Simon's operational stewardship, Co-opportunity was forced to grow up when he retired. That transition point could have doomed the Co-op, as it has for a number of other co-ops. As a Board, we labored over the process of General Manager succession, but ultimately landed on an "insider" with the promotion of Bruce Palma.

Our instincts proved right, as Bruce has led a steady march of professionalizing our management structure. Bruce and his management team have created systems that prodded staff to higher productivity and more accountability. They have done that with a keen ear to keeping the unique community and atmosphere that defines the Co-op difference. Although the store has better products, better profit margins and better service, it still has that funky, diverse and homey quality that distinguishes it from the panoply of Whole Foods arrayed around it.

As Will moved on, the Board had to grow up, too. No longer could we just defer to his assurances that all was well at the Co-op. Instead, we joined a national trend and moved to a policy governance model. Although it seemed somewhat artificial and semantic at first, it has allowed us to focus more on strategic planning than operational meddling. The monitoring process has actually allowed us to oversee management much more efficiently and critically, and the ends definition in our policies has allowed us to coalesce behind a triple-bottom line strategic vision. As I became President right as we implemented the change, I can remember us all struggling to understand what our new role was in the first few years. But it is a pleasure to see that most of our meetings now are much more productive and interesting and "out of the weeds."

And we have now become major players in the national cooperative movement. Bruce moved enthusiastically to join the NCG, and his staff now takes full advantage of all the training and best practices it offers. That integration has introduced us to many co-op consultants who have helped both management and the Board refine and improve their practices. The Board has become more committed and enthusiastic about attending CCMA and encouraging cooperation with other cooperatives. And we have tried to shepherd more local co-op growth through our financial and other support for the nascent Arroyo Food Co-op.

This decade-long transition positions us well for a vibrant future. The organization has coalesced around a vision of Good Growth. Expanding the Co-op and all the advantages it brings to the local community, the owners and the staff to more places in our city. I can imagine 10 years from now a chain of five Co-ops with pure, trusted products, great-tasting delis, and cutting-edge new products. And it will be operated for a decent profit by a professional staff, and a strategic, watchful Board who continue to improve with the help of friends around the Co-op Country.

Jens B. Koepke, Co-opportunity Board Member and President (2000-)

Serving on the board of Co-opportunity provided me with my first chance to help guide a business enterprise, albeit one with a social as well as a commercial purpose. Working with David Thompson, Ruth Goldway and others, I played a small part in helping Co-opportunity to deal with internal strife and smooth out its management operation so that it could survive and prosper.

My practical experience with Co-opportunity in Santa Monica gave me ideas and information which I put to good use when President Carter appointed me to the founding board of the National Cooperative Bank in Washington, D.C. Working with David Thompson on a national level, I helped to populate the top management of the bank with talented co-op entrepreneurs and managers from around the country.

Ambassador Derek Shearer Chevalier Professor of Diplomacy; Director, McKinnon Center for Global Affairs, Occidental College

FOREWORD

Congratulations to Co-opportunity on its 41st anniversary. The co-op has earned and maintained support from its community by growing and responding to the constancy of changing demands. From its early days, Co-opportunity has led the awakening toward a more sustainable future in food and agriculture.

Co-opportunity, as it went from buying club to store, from almost bankruptcy to success, from a loose-knit and collective decision-making structure to a board of directors, is the story of every retail food co-op in the 1970s and 80s. Those decades were a time of sea change in how Americans thought about food, agricultural practices and the environment. They were also the decades California cuisine was born.

David J. Thompson's history, with its facts, figures and personal recollections, recounts the many ways in which Co-opportunity was the Southern California beachhead during the transformative years of 1970 – 1990, when California's cooperative laws and farmers market regulations were changed, a national infrastructure for debt financing was created for consumer cooperatives and food retailing was radically changed to reflect the burgeoning environmental and health ethic fueled by books such as Rachel Carson's "Silent Spring" and Frances Moore Lappe's "Diet for a Small Planet."

The creation of a California cuisine is not only the story of chefs breaking free from traditional recipes and strictures and cooking with local ingredients in season. Nor is it only the story of restaurateurs who experimented with open kitchens and new wine lists. As Thompson so well demonstrates, it is also the story of the 150 or more retail cooperatives like Co-opportunity, which charted new retail and legal territory to bring a new kind of food to everyday people at home.

These intrepid food co-ops pioneered much of what major retailers now practice commonly -- the sale of unprocessed whole grains, oils and nuts in bulk, cheese hand cut, organic produce of new and different varietals, sustainably raised meats and specialty meats. Through the co-ops, these items became available for the first time and provisioned people cooking at home, packing school lunches, and preparing dishes to share at community and church potlucks. These co-ops helped create the system, wholesale and distribution that fueled the quiet revolution taking place on farms and in restaurants that became California cuisine.

Why did co-op leaders such as Thompson and those he so ably credits in his expansive history, donate thousands of volunteer hours over several decades to build these community-based, cooperative businesses? Perhaps for the same reasons leaders around the world have done so for centuries – need.

The marketplace was not meeting the needs of consumers who wanted healthier, unprocessed foods, who wanted to support a market for the newly created small and organic farming movement, who had a vision for a more environmentally sustainable way of eating and conducting business. For the most part, the leaders met these needs through the creation of an economically democratic system. Later, many for-profit natural food businesses and even major retailers would emulate the changes pioneered by the food cooperatives, bringing them to scale, changing the system.

These early co-op leaders had a vision and a dream that seemingly, in the space of one decade, the 1970s, was felt throughout California, the United States, and across northern Europe and England. In short, people collectively pursued a food retailing revolution, the cooperative way. There were no models then. As Thompson states, cooperators sometimes violated laws and regulations in the process of building their businesses.

Like so many food co-ops, Co-opportunity had met its need for capital in part through the sale of shares. It had done so, unknowingly without a permit from the Department of Corporations, to expand the store, buy stock, create a wholesale produce company. These co-ops started small, often in the form of buying clubs such as Co-opportunity's Westside Buyers Club, and grew the only way a business can without major infusions of capital – organically, stage-by-stage and step-by-step. They were so small; they essentially flew under the system's radar.

Co-opportunity and its sister food cooperatives, as well as the complex web of trucking companies, wholesalers, food processors and agricultural producers that fed into the retail system and were supported by it, did not build their early success at entrepreneurship solely on technical skills. It was a collective leadership, both internally to Co-opportunity and throughout California and across the nation; of visionary risk-takers who sought not to make a profit for themselves, but to create an economic democracy while at the same time create a peaceful food revolution.

Their vision propelled them to take big risks. Their ability to change and respond, to analyze problems and seize opportunities, created the momentum that allowed those with technical skills to help build these retail businesses. The early founders felt at liberty to collectively pursue and materialize their vision without permission from others, without trying to change what was, but to build their businesses as a model for the world as much as to meet their needs for, as the International Slow Food movement later termed it, clean, safe and delicious food.

Having participated in the creation of its history, Thompson takes us through the roots of Co-opportunity in its predecessor, the Santa Monica Co-op, whose failure to respond to the changing marketplace brought about the closure of its store and provided an important cautionary tale for Co-opportunity. Reflecting back on those years, an unmistakably shared characteristic of the leadership was one of self-help, learning from failure, never giving up.

Leaders were not lawyers, accountants, and by and large not of the professional class. They were not of the system. In spite of that, or more directly perhaps because of that, they laid claim to and demanded changes in state and federal regulations and laws that governed the system. Yet power only yields to power. Co-opportunity served as the southern California hub, signature-gathering base, to influence elected leaders from that populace area in the state legislature and Congress. Co-opportunity became a base of power for the changes sought.

As Thompson outlines, Co-opportunity assisted in every major governmental change, from the three-year process to carve out regulations for Certified Farmers Markets to new "blue sky" laws within the Department of Corporations to a definition of the term organic at the state level in California, to the multi-year, multi-cooperative sector effort to create the National Consumer Cooperative Bank. Each change conceptualized not in backrooms and through idle ideological discussion, but in boardroom lofts and in storerooms and grocery aisles.

Each change sought was based on concrete problems and impediments to success, therein perhaps, providing a persuasive part of the argument for change. These food cooperatives accomplished a great deal in 20 years, providing a foundation for much of the growth in food cooperatives that has occurred in the decades since.

Thompson provides a link for those interested in cooperatives today to the past, from the Rochdale Pioneers of England in the Industrial Revolution, to the beginning of Co-opportunity in California in the environmental movement. Yet this tale is much more than the story of the little store that could, or even one store whose leaders such as Thompson had a radical impact on food retailing nationally.

This is the story of the way in which community economic development, the good neighbor principal put onto Main Street, created a legacy. Co-opportunity grew sister organizations such as the Santa Monica Farmers Market, other co-op stores such as Venice Ocean Park Food Commonwealth (VOP Co-op), political leaders who went from the co-op board to the City Council, and breakthrough environmental yet pragmatic legislation such as the first in the nation Bottle Bill, and now commonplace concepts such as direct marketing from farmers to retailers.

I commend Thompson on documenting this everyday history of a community, in this case Santa Monica, but from my vantage point then in the first Governor Jerry Brown Administration as Cooperative Development Program Manager, a story similar to communities up and down California, from Arcata to San Diego and within the great Central Valley from Redding to Irvine. Indeed, across the nation. The story Thompson tells us is timeless, which is why it is so compelling. It is not a fable or fairytale, yet it has good and evil, success and failure. It is the story of a group of people who shared a vision, a dream, and collectively manifested their vision on the material plane for the betterment of all.

Ann M. Evans is co-founder Davis Food Co-op and Davis Farmers Market, former Cooperative Development Director in the Department of Consumer Affairs for the State of California, and a former Mayor, City of Davis.

"Filled with unforgettable characters and atmospheric details, Thompson's Co-opportunity chronicle tells an inspiring tale of community dedication to a common goal. Though set in California, the events have been repeated in scores of communities since the early 1970s. Coming out of the civil rights and anti-war activism of the 1960s, people throughout the country have learned that working together they could make significant and lasting change. Thompson's rich story makes you want to join a co-op just to hang out with these remarkable people who support community-owned businesses.**"**

Ann Hoyt, Cooperative Hall of Fame Inductee 2015, former Chair, National Cooperative Business Association, CCMA Superstar

INTRODUCTION
BY DAVID J. THOMPSON

You have in your hands the kind of history that is seldom published. It is the history of ordinary people achieving an unordinary purpose. Co-opportunity, the largest and longest running food cooperative in Los Angeles County, is owned and controlled by its 10,000 members. It has the highest sales per square foot of any food co-op in the USA and has higher sales per square foot than Whole Foods.

There is no other grocery store in Los Angeles County like it. It is the only retail store in the County that uses a patronage refund system to share its profits with its members. The majority of its owners live within three miles of the store. No other LA store is more locally owned than Co-opportunity.

This is a story of hope, persistence and achievement. It is the story of scores of board members, a few general managers, hundreds of staff and thousands of members. It is the story of cooperation, opportunity and unity, all encompassed in our name - Co-opportunity. It is the story of reciprocity and solidarity urged by the Cooperative Principles of the International Cooperative Alliance.

It is a story of thanks to all of the people who have made Co-opportunity what it is today. Every reader of this book will be someone who contributed something to Co-opportunity in the past and is about to contribute something to our future.

This story is meant for four audiences:

1. For all of us who are Co-opportunity. To remind the members, customers and staff of Co-opportunity from whence we started and how we laid a foundation for today - knowing our history is a strength for building tomorrow.

2. For other similar co-ops of the "new wave" era. To remind thousands of other people who started their cooperatives in the same era of how proud they should be of the "new wave" cooperatives around the USA. You, too, were started in a similar way and as we've grown stronger, we have united in our

joint efforts. The National Co+op Grocers is our finest example of working together. Thank you for being one of the 150 other food co-ops we align ourselves with every day.

3. For the "old wave" co-ops like the Santa Monica Co-op, Associated Cooperatives and the Twin Pines Cooperative Foundation, who laid the groundwork, shared their model and their resources and who bequeathed their assets of ideas and inspiration.

4. And lastly, for the people who are building the "third wave" of new cooperatives being developed and opened in this new millennium. We dedicate this book to you: To the many new food co-ops in formation at this time. To those of you engaged in those lengthy meetings and incessant member drives. By reading this book, you will know that much more is possible than you could imagine and much more can be done than you believe. So, too, will that co-op store and beloved community you wish to see become real, because we are here to tell you that it will happen. We will help you in every way possible and wish you well in joining us to build a model cooperative economy. We also commend the Food Co-op Initiative and its many supporters for their great work.

During its 41st Anniversary Year, Co-opportunity will achieve over $24 million in sales to over 2,000 people a day, have over 10,000 members, and be the employer of over 100 people. Together we have accomplished a lot. Others will add their voice to this book, taking pride in sharing their present achievements and future hopes for Co-opportunity.

Co-opportunity is unique. In an era when we are led to believe that ordinary people cannot and should not enter into business together, we are a successful self-made enterprise that is self-capitalized by our members.

We do not act to gain profit by our investment, but that our investment would fund our shared goals about food and community. We seek a better world. We wish to merge idealism and practicality and follow where our mission, enterprise and hopes take us. We are stewards of the people's business and will carefully grow to serve others who wish to join us in our efforts. We're in it for the long haul.

As far as I know, of the 100s of food cooperatives started in the 1970s, and beyond, there are only a few that have published books about their beginnings. I believe it critical to keep a record of the history of ordinary people. Otherwise, where can people learn that there is so much we can do by working together to achieve common purpose? If we know of the achievements of others before us, we can gain confidence in beginning anew.

When we began in 1974, there were perhaps 50 "old wave" consumer cooperatives in the USA. Almost all of them had begun in the 1930s, during the Depression. However in 2015, there are only about five of those "old wave" co-ops still in existence. By getting past our 41st birthday and remaining vibrant, just like the over 100 "new wave" food co-ops started in our same era, Co-opportunity will flourish into a new era of our choosing.

As a member of the National Co+op Grocers (NCG), Co-opportunity participates in a national business services cooperative for retail food co-ops located throughout the United States. NCG represents over 150 food co-ops operating 200 stores in 38 states with combined annual sales of over $1.6 billion with over 1.3 million member-owners.

Most of those 150 cooperatives are our peers in terms of starting in the same era, seeking the same goals and going into business. We share a great deal with each other and even more every year. Our histories are similar but this history of Co-opportunity is one of the few histories which have been put into print.

Enjoy what was created for you, and by your actions, strengthen Co-opportunity for today and pass it on in good health to the members of tomorrow.

AND NOW FOR A ROBUST ROUND OF "GRATEFULNESS"

To the farmers who give us such great gifts from the earth and the suppliers that truly care about their products.

To the National Co+op Grocers, the National Cooperative Business Association, Associated Cooperatives and Twin Pines Cooperative Foundation, CDS Consulting Co-op, Consumers Cooperative Management Association (CCMA), and the entire family of cooperatives who imbue us with reciprocity, solidarity and unity in all we do.

To so many people - for all you gave, are giving and will give. Thanks to all the board members for protecting Co-opportunity and planning for tomorrow. Thanks to Will Simon and Bruce Palma for being great general managers through all the day-to-day activities that ensure our success. Thanks to the staff who work so hard from before dawn and after dusk to provide us with a great experience. And a big thank you to all you members and customers for your loyalty, support and capital.

Co-opportunity would not be what it is without the contribution of all of you.

Whatever is in our future, we can walk toward it in unity, because we are strengthened by our past and stronger together.

In gratitude, admiration and cooperation,

David J. Thompson,
Co-Founder Co-opportunity

"Thompson's deep knowledge of co-operative history; his vast personal experience; and his insights on community organizing add enormously to this absorbing history of Co-opportunity. This is a well-told story about successful and constructive community collaboration in a heady time of social change. It offers cooperatives as a significant, realistic and people-centered option for communities recovering from the Great Recession.**"**

Ann Hoyt, Cooperative Hall of Fame Inductee 2015, former Chair, National Cooperative Business Association, CCMA Superstar

"David always brings the highest degree of integrity to whatever he is working on. He never sought the "fame or fortune" that blinds so many others. He has never lost sight of the reasons for doing what he did - to empower others; to show folks how to have a greater say in their own lives, in their own choices and to bring out the best in people.

To many in the California Legislature, David is "Mr. Co-op." To me, he's all that and more. But most importantly David is one of my longest and dearest friends. **"**

Richard Katz, former California Assembly Democratic Leader, California Assembly Member (1980-1996)

"David Thompson is a vital resource in chronicling the history of the cooperative movement. He has written a book that should be read by the next wave of cooperators who now follow in the footsteps of the Co-opportunity founders. It is a book that can inspire their work. **"**

Terry Appleby, General Manager, Hanover Consumer Cooperative Society, Past Chair, National Co+op™ Grocers Board of Directors (2014)

CHAPTER 1
A STORY OF STARTING CO-OPPORTUNITY: THE BEGINNING YEARS

Entering the 21st Century, Co-opportunity ranks as one of the most successful consumer cooperatives in the USA, and by square foot, the highest volume natural foods co-op store in the country.

Running an attractive store in the sun-blessed City of Santa Monica, Co-opportunity has become a local community treasure and a nationally recognized cooperative organization.

Through the longtime leadership of General Manager, Bruce Palma, the former General Manager, Will Simon, a talented staff and the steady hands of a series of committed boards during the past two decades, Co-opportunity has entered a phase of maturity, growth and opportunity.

Co-opportunity now has an assured future after rising from Chapter 11 (bankruptcy) in the 1980s into today's financially strong and well-managed organization.

With its present strength, Co-opportunity now has the ability to resource the next new chapter of our cooperative. In its 41st year, Co-opportunity looms to emulate other natural foods cooperatives around the country.

From our humble, frugal beginnings, Co-opportunity has emerged to join NCG, a network of over 150 other food co-ops around the country that operate almost 200 stores in 38 states.

Within a few years after Co-opportunity's birth in 1974, our co-op had become one of the most dynamic in the country. The 1970s were an era of immense change in attitudes toward food and farming, with our co-op at the forefront.

Co-opportunity's leaders and supportive membership played an important role in passing legislation which established Certified Farmers' Markets, Direct Marketing and Organic Certification and farming methods in California. Co-opportunity's early efforts ultimately led to the creation of the now world famous Santa Monica Farmers Market.

Co-opportunity helped lay the groundwork for the Venice Ocean Park Co-op and supported efforts to create cooperative housing in the city.

We also impacted co-ops throughout the state and nationally with our leadership on state legislation relating to cooperative corporations, cooperative capitalization and the establishment of the National Cooperative Bank and the National Cooperative Bank Development Corporation. There were many out-of-date regulatory barriers in California to be broken and Co-opportunity was there to make a major difference.

In 2015, Co-opportunity celebrated its 41st birthday and with that comes thoughts about how a humble co-op got started. Cooperation is the ability of people to come together democratically, to unite their capital and resources and to go into business to meet their needs. Behind every exciting future, there is a past full of struggle, and Co-opportunity is no exception. The history of every democratic enterprise is the untold story of ordinary people doing unordinary things.

A cooperative is, after all, people in search of progress towards meeting their needs. Co-opportunity's development, like all group activity, is a story of dozens of board members, a handful of managers, hundreds of committed activists and thousands of supportive members. For them and the hundreds of staff members, it is a story of unique success against unusual odds.

Co-opportunity began as a copy of a Canadian idea called Direct Charge, open only to members, with every member required to do work shifts. The original Direct Charge model was changed substantially along the way, but the cooperative form and purpose has remained.

Were Co-opportunity to have been a private business, there were enough difficulties over the past 41 years to have time and again ensured failure. If Co-opportunity had been a small business, it would by now have failed and been forgotten. We would not be here to talk about what happened.

Yet, being a cooperative, with a goal of service above profit, the co-op and its members weathered adversity, rose above catastrophe and emerged intact, sober and wiser. That is how we got where we are, but let's not forget where we came from. To know Co-opportunity's history, one must first look at the history of another era and actually at another cooperative organization.

"In this narrative, Thompson also makes important connections between "old wave" cooperatives and the ascendance of the "new wave"—something that has been little explored in food co-op chronicles. Additionally, Thompson pays homage to Toyohiko Kagawa, the deeply influential Japanese cooperator who was considered co-father of many California cooperatives.**"**

Patricia Cumbie, author of "Growing with Purpose, Forty Years of Seward Community Cooperative"

"Like its peers, Co-opportunity was born out of the ideas and philosophies of the 1960s, with a deep passion for equality, social justice, and to making whole foods available to its members. This set off a quiet revolution in what eventually became the "natural foods" industry.**"**

Karen Zimbelman, Director of Membership and Cooperative Relations, National Co+op™ Grocers

CHAPTER 2
CALIFORNIA CO-OPS, THE DEPRESSION, WORLD WAR II AND BEYOND

Without a doubt the most important seed for Co-opportunity was the old Consumer Cooperative Society of Santa Monica (CCSSM), commonly called the Santa Monica Co-op, whose first store was at 5th and Pico. Incorporated on March 24, 1935, by a group of local Christian leaders and Depression era social activists, the Santa Monica Co-op was an attempt to lessen the burden of the Depression.

Many of the original members of the co-op were Methodists who had been inspired by the teachings and speeches of the great Japanese Christian and Co-op leader, Toyohiko Kagawa. Kagawa had often spoken in Santa Monica and Los Angeles in the 1930s, drawing large crowds. He so impacted people on the Westside that there is a Kagawa Street in Pacific Palisades named after him. Because he received so much continued support from the Los Angeles area's Christians and social activists, Kagawa named one of the buildings at his Osaka Settlement House in Japan, "Los Angeles Hall." The building still stands.

The co-op wave of the 1930s and 40s was also fueled by the practical idealism of people like the populist writer, Upton Sinclair. In 1906, Sinclair had founded Helicon Home Colony, a utopia based on cooperative principles in New Jersey, from the proceeds of his best selling novel, "The Jungle." Gaylord Wilshire (for whom Wilshire Boulevard is named) was the Treasurer of the Colony.

Sinclair ran for Governor of California in 1934 on the EPIC (End Poverty in California) program. He ran on a platform that placed major emphasis on self-help co-ops. Because of the strong support in the Santa Monica community, Sinclair declared his candidacy for Governor of California in Santa Monica at the Miramar Hotel, which still stands at the corner of Wilshire Boulevard and Ocean Avenue.

Sinclair won the Democratic Party nomination, but his progressive platform scared the powers that be in California. Different influential power groups undermined his candidacy and stealth-funded his opponents. Some regard Sinclair's 1934 race as the birth of modern campaigning with its dirty tricks, smear campaign, unethical tactics and hidden spending. Even so, Sinclair still came in a strong second in a very competitive three-person race for Governor.

The Director of the End Poverty League and advocate of cooperatives who worked on Sinclair's campaign was a young Jerry Voorhis. Jerry Voorhis was swept into the California Assembly by support from EPIC. If Sinclair had won, cooperatives would have been one of the main forces for economic revival of California.

In 1936, after the grueling campaign, Sinclair wrote a novel called "Co-op" that became a best seller. The novel detailed the hard work put in by residents of a Southern California coastal community (based upon both Santa Barbara and Santa Monica), which fought to start and hold together their co-op to help themselves through the hard times.

Upon arriving in California in 1915, Sinclair had set about organizing a consumers' cooperative in Pasadena, where he lived, and helped to organize the Pacific Cooperative League. Sinclair's commitment to cooperatives lasted his entire adult life.

After election to the California Assembly in 1934, Jerry Voorhis was immediately elected to Congress in 1936, from the Pomona area and became a constant proponent of cooperatives. Regretfully, Voorhis was defeated in 1947, by Richard Nixon in a dirty campaign that first established Nixon's underhanded techniques.

Voorhis went on to become the Executive Director (1947-1967) of the Cooperative League of the USA (CLUSA), now called the National Cooperative Business Association (NCBA). Until his death in 1984, Jerry never forgot the strong support he received from the cooperators of Santa Monica and, in fact, spoke at a number of the annual meetings of the Santa Monica Co-op.

Voorhis' last speaking engagement in the Santa Monica area was at a fundraiser in 1978, at the Ocean Park Methodist Church for the Venice-Ocean Park Co-op. Reverend Jim Conn had graciously made the balcony of the Church available to us. Even at 77, Voorhis was willing to drive 100 miles at night to speak to a small group of people wanting to start a co-op. Jerry had terrible asthma and to climb the steps to the top of the Church was quite painful – but he did it.

With its beginnings in the Depression, the Santa Monica Co-op was one of the few consumer cooperatives in the Los Angeles area to last beyond the Second World War. One by one, the other consumer co-ops in the Los Angeles area (Hollywood Co-op, Zone 26 Co-op and the Whittier Co-op) passed away until the Santa Monica Co-op was the last one remaining in Southern California. Although the Santa Monica Co-op moved from Santa Monica to open a store in 1948 at 2021 S. Barrington Avenue in West Los Angeles, it always retained Santa Monica in its name.

Thankfully, a core group of believers kept the consumer co-op flag flying in Southern California. The Co-op maintained the store, but with increasingly marginal returns. It was the continued increase in the underlying value of the land in West Los Angeles that helped keep the Co-op afloat.

The Santa Monica Co-op's eye to the wider co-op world took place through its membership in Associated Cooperatives (AC). AC was started in 1935, to meet the wholesale and service needs of the growing retail cooperatives. The Santa Monica Co-op joined AC in 1940, to take advantage of the group's buying activities. As the consumer co-op sector grew, AC was able to extend its trucking network to Southern California.

AFTER WORLD WAR II

When the war ended, growth in many forms came to Southern California. The new co-op store in West Los Angeles benefitted from the population growth on the Westside and the soaring post-war economy.

Yet one particular activity at that time, fostered by the Santa Monica Co-op, would have major national impact on housing policy, cooperative living and race relations.

Among the critical issues of the day were the need to build housing for the returning veterans and their young families. But the rising cost of land, the lack of equity and access to the short supply of building materials made it impossible for the young families to own a home.

A group of the members of the Santa Monica Co-op took matters into their own hands. At the Santa Monica core were four veterans who were also musicians. Together in 1946, they formed the Mutual Housing Association (MHA). One of the four, Leonard Krupnick, was also a board member of the Santa Monica Co-op and of Associated Cooperatives. Others who joined the Mutual Housing Association had strong links to the cooperative movement.

The Co-op core wanted to build a cooperative community where returning veterans and others of all races and religions could live together in harmony. Their small group grew quickly to over 500 families. They enthusiastically pooled their funds together and bought a huge swath of eight hundred acres of land in what is today Crestwood Hills in Brentwood.

The MHA immediately joined Associated Cooperatives to be alongside the Santa Monica Co-op in all things cooperative in California. But there was a practical angle, as a regional wholesaler for both consumer and agricultural cooperatives, Associated Cooperatives had priority access to the needed building materials and lumber.

This chapter in the history of the Santa Monica Co-op is told vividly in a recent book by Cory Buckner entitled, "Crestwood Hills: The Chronicle of a Modern Utopia."

Wendy Krupnick (daughter of Leonard and Jean Krupnick) remembers that her father was proud of the community they built against the odds, but disappointed that the full aims of racial inclusion could not at that time be achieved. The dream of a post world war cooperative utopia was not then to be.

Regretfully, the Federal Housing Agency (FHA) was opposed to cooperative ownership of almost anything and would not approve the group financing of the planned community. Without FHA approval, the project would fail, so the entire cooperative infrastructure and dream of shared ownership had to be jettisoned. The five hundred families had to accept that their utopia was now to be an ordinary sub-division with a shared playground and a few other cooperative elements.

But the members' troubles were not yet over. After all those changes to become a sub-division acceptable to the FHA, the co-op had to disband and only individual ownership of each of the lots was allowed. The next step by FHA then killed the inter-racial dreams of the founders. The FHA would not finance any home anywhere in the USA unless they carried in the title a racial covenant that restricted occupancy only to persons who are White or Caucasian. This prevented the lots being sold to minorities. Many of the MHA's Crestwood Hills homes still carry that racial covenant in their deed. Here is the covenant as #11.

MUTUAL HOUSING ASSOCIATION, INC., a California corporation hereinafter referred to as "the Corporation," hereby declares:

1. That it is the owner of the following property, to wit:

Lots 1 to 197, inclusive, of Tract 14944 In the City of Los Angeles, County of Los Angeles, State of California, as per map recorded in Book #346 Pages 39-45 of Maps, in the office of the County recorder of said County.

11., That no part of any lot in said Tract shall ever be, at any time, used or occupied by any person not of the White or Caucasian race, excepting such as are actually employed as servants or employees upon such lot by the owners or tenants thereof actually residing thereon.

However, in the late 1940s, Thurgood Marshall (later of the Supreme Court) was able to convince President Truman to end by Executive Order all racial discrimination in housing financed by the FHA. Thurgood Marshall, who himself, could not own a home due to racial covenants in NYC, legally represented the efforts of a number of housing cooperatives to bring an end to racial discrimination. Indeed, Marshall's first home ownership was a 1950s membership in the Morningside Heights Cooperative in NYC.

The Executive Order came too late to save the inclusive interracial dreams of the founders of three housing cooperatives; Mutual Housing Association in Brentwood, Community Homes in Reseda and Peninsula Homes Association in Ladera created by the Palo Alto Co-op.

But the legal and political efforts of these three co-ops and others around the country ensured that racial discrimination by FHA would legally come to an end in 1948, for everyone in the USA. Thanks to the particular efforts of US housing cooperatives, all races were finally eligible to own a home financed by the FHA.

The three cooperative communities are still studied by urban planners as critical elements of the post war urban era. What they had in common with Santa Monica Co-op was that the three cooperative communities were all members of Associated Cooperatives.

Through its membership in Associated Cooperatives, the Santa Monica Co-op was able to attend the annual AC meetings, receive the regular publication of Cooperative Leadership, and send its members to Co-op Camp Sierra. By the 1960s, this was Santa Monica's only door to the co-op world. The avenue would later prove to be one of the keys to Co-opportunity's future.

With the 1960s, came the civil rights marches, the anti-war movement and change in the air. I was attending Santa Monica Community College (where I was one of the leaders of the campus anti-war movement). In 1968, I ran for student body President on an anti-war ticket. An artist/surfer won on a platform of having "fun in the sun." A returned Vietnam Vet came in second. I placed third. How, you may ask, could an immigrant who was not a citizen succeed in efforts to change government policies? "Those were the days, my friend..."

I helped organize over 400 students from Santa Monica College and other junior colleges in LA County to go to San Francisco to participate in the Peace March. At the peak of one of the hills during our march, I looked at the tens of thousands in front and behind me, and wondered how many marches there would have to be until peace came. I realized I wanted to be engaged in building an economy for peace on a daily basis rather than marching every time there was a war.

I returned to Santa Monica with the idea that what the world needed to end war was a cooperative economy. I remembered from my activist youth in England that the consumer co-ops in Britain had played a major role in the peace movement, the anti-nuclear movement and the anti-apartheid movement.

I was born in Blackpool, England, on June 2, 1942. My first memory is of war. Four months earlier on February 2, 1942, Graham Nash was born just five minutes' walk away. The lyrics of Nash's song, "Military Madness," about being born in Blackpool during the war ring true with me.

At fifteen, I attended the first Aldermaston March protest in Trafalgar Square in London on Easter Friday in 1958. This was the moment when the "Peace Sign" was first unveiled to the world. Gerald Holtom's now ubiquitous design was revealed in black and white on placards.

The Campaign for Nuclear Disarmament (CND) sprung from that march. There were perhaps 10,000 of us at the demonstration, none of whom had any idea that we were witnessing many firsts, including an enduring symbol that continues to be a witness to history today.

For me, however, it was the role of cooperatives in the peace movement that made the greatest impression. The meetings that brought about the march and boosted the movement were often held at cooperative halls. In particular, the Co-operative Women's Guilds were one of the foster parents of CND and the march. The leaflets handed out at the march were published for free by the London Co-operative Society (LCS). The loudspeakers and equipment were also supplied by the LCS. Perhaps most importantly for the marchers, the Co-operative provided a van that went to Aldermaston at the front of the march, as rapid support for the needs of ten thousand marchers on a fifty mile journey. That co-op van became an iconic leader of the first march and many more following.

There was a Cooperative Way. I saw it in London in my youth and wanted to be part of creating it in America as well.

"Those of us supporting new co-op development owe a debt of gratitude for everything co-ops like Co-opportunity have done to pave the way. The idealism, commitment, and tireless effort of their founders and members continue to inspire us. Thanks to David Thompson, storyteller and historian, for reminding us of our roots and honoring the people whose vision leads to our cooperative future.**"**

Stuart Reid, Executive Director, Food Co-op Initiative

CHAPTER 3
THE CRITICAL ROLE OF THE SANTA MONICA CO-OP

While living previously on Granville Avenue in West Los Angeles, I frequently passed a store with a big "Co-op" sign on the roof. One day, I went looking for that store and found it at 2021 S. Barrington Avenue. It was a little dark, old fashioned and rather foreboding inside. All that, however, was put to rest by the appearance of a smiling and very dapper elderly gentleman dressed to the nines in a dark suit, starched collar and carefully knotted tie.

He was George Campbell. When he asked if he could help me, I asked him, "Is this Co-op connected with the ones in England?"

"Yes," he said, enthusiastically. "We are linked with the co-op that started in Rochdale, Lancashire in 1844."

Then I uttered a few simple words that would forever change the direction of my life. "Well, I was born near Rochdale!"

"In that case," said George, "you must serve on the Board."

(When my cousins from Rochdale (Vera and Pat) learned that I had claimed I was born near Rochdale, they laughed heartily. Blackpool is less than fifty miles from Rochdale, which is regarded as "near" in the US, whereas, my Rochdale cousins make it quite clear that Blackpool is nowhere near Rochdale.)

In 1969, at 27, I became the youngest elected member of the Board whose average age was over 60. I found an organization with plenty of commitment to cooperatives, but of limited energy.

In the 1950s, the Co-op had moved from Santa Monica to Barrington Avenue, which was still an agricultural part of West Los Angeles back then, so it could also operate a Farmers Market. Japanese-American farmers had recently returned to their Westside truck farms from the internment camps.

Seven blocks east of the Co-op at Sawtelle Blvd. and Olympic Blvd. was and still is the heart of the Westside Japanese-American community. The two blocks on Sawtelle contain numerous Japanese restaurants, nurseries and businesses serving the Japanese-American population. For several decades, that part of Sawtelle was also home to the West Los Angeles Japanese Credit Union. Many of the Japanese-American families were also members of the Santa Monica Co-op.

Those Japanese-American families remembered with gratitude that Associated Cooperatives had established a co-op store in nine of the ten internment camps. The AC-supplied Co-op store at Manzanar in California was the second largest consumer cooperative in America in 1943. Camp cooperatives that served over 100,000 internees were the primary way supplies were distributed. After the war, many of the internees who worked at the camp co-ops would later find welcome employment in California's consumer cooperatives.

The district west of Sawtelle was subsequently zoned industrial with few people living nearby. Without the outstanding loyalty of the co-op's members, the Co-op would have gone out of business.

I believed, however, that the Cooperative Way was the true path and set about recruiting like-minded people to be on committees and to run for the board. One-by-one, a younger set of leaders was elected to the board, although we never held a majority. Nevertheless, with an active board minority, coupled with our energy and interests, we began to make changes.

For example, the co-op had a large unused parking lot. We arranged to have Israel Feuer set up the Westside Recycling Center there for people to bring their newspapers for recycling. Every Saturday, Israel and his crew and a few co-op volunteers would hand-load tons of paper into truck beds, which were then picked up by a regular truck. Week after week, however, the Center received more paper than it sent out. The local Fire Chief warned the Center that we were creating a fire danger. Often times, the Center needed to pay truckers to haul away the surplus paper. The Center would receive cash payments that it used to pay for its publications and outreach programs.

I can tell you, it was a hard, backbreaking way to save the world! Looking at a ten foot high mass of newspaper all day was dispiriting. The Center finally had to close down because waste paper was continuing to take over the parking spaces at the back of the Co-op. In 1998, Israel Feuer ran for Secretary of State on the Peace and Freedom ticket.

Our activist group turned the large, neglected upstairs meeting room at the Co-op back over to education activities. We organized a speaker series about health, food and the environment. We sorted all the great classic co-op books hidden in the cupboards into a more accessible library on cooperatives, food and health issues. Adelle Davis and her philosophy on the health attributes of food were then the favorite of the old-time cooperators. Consumer activist and KPFK radio show host, Ida Honoroff, gave a number of well-attended lectures at the Co-op. We strengthened the annual meeting as a part of our attempt to revive the cooperative. In addition, we brought out a regular co-op newsletter.

We also pushed the advantages of co-op membership, because people who joined the Co-op were eligible to join the Santa Monica Consumers' Credit Union (founded in 1944), which had its offices at the Co-op. The leadership of the credit union were always great supporters of the Co-op. Belva Roberts, the longtime CU manager, was a strong voice for cooperatives within the credit union movement. Other CU board members such as Al Trumpler (longtime co-op board member whose mother was one of the first board members of the Berkeley Co-op) and Fernando Sendejas (longtime GM of the Co-op) all played different roles in the Co-op. There were many others who gave to both organizations. In 2015, Fernando and Belva continue to serve on the board of the Santa Monica Consumers Cooperative.

Through the Santa Monica Co-op's contacts with Associated Cooperatives, we were able to make contacts with the kindred generation of younger leaders. AC introduced us to leaders at Berkeley, Palo Alto and the University Cooperative Association at Berkeley, as well as the other natural food co-op buying groups and small food co-op stores throughout the state. The AC publication, Cooperative Leadership, was immensely valuable as a dispenser of information about the consumer cooperative sector.

Within the store, we began to change the old fashioned merchandising style. We pushed for more vegetarian products, more organic produce and a larger line of health foods. Fernando Sendejas came in as a competent young manager who earnestly wanted to shift the product line. In this, Fernando supplemented the work of Bruce Mower, the produce manager who had made changes to reflect the growing interest in organic produce.

We were also able to attract two butchers -Vic and Ken - to come to the Co-op and re-focus the department on meat products such as free-range chicken and beef without chemicals. (Vic and Ken eventually left the Co-op to run the meat counter within the first Mrs. Gooch's store located in West LA, which opened in 1977). Mrs. Gooch's was taken over by Whole Foods in 1993, and that store became the first Whole Foods store in Los Angeles.

The next step was to convert an area of the store into a health food section. That space attracted a younger crowd as the products represented a changing attitude toward health, the use of land, and farming methods. The change, however, seemed to come with difficulty as the board politely resisted responding fully to changing food habits. Our group was ahead of its time, but the organization had a limited tolerance and resources for change. One of my most regrettable moments in co-op life was to assess soberly that the Santa Monica Co-op would not be able to change.

Happily, the Santa Monica Consumers Credit Union (SMCCU) under the leadership of Belva Roberts, the CEO and their board members, was able to live on after the closure of the Barrington store. Membership in the Credit Union was only available to members of the Consumers Cooperative Society of Santa Monica, so the leaders of SMCCU worked hand-in-hand with the Co-op board to assure that the organization lived on even after the store closed. The Santa Monica Co-op was possibly the only "old wave" co-op in California that closed while in the black.

For the next fifteen years, SMCCU operated as a stand alone credit union at 1044 Pico Boulevard in Santa Monica, by serving select employee groups (SEGs) on the Westside. In the year 2000, however, SMCCU entered into a merger with the Kinecta Federal Credit Union (formerly Hughes Aircraft Employees Credit Union founded in 1940). Becoming a member of the Santa Monica Co-op is one avenue available for joining Kinecta. As a result, the CCSSM still continues to operate as a cooperative in the State of California. www.ccssm.org

The Consumers Cooperative Society of Santa Monica is the oldest, continuing consumer cooperative in California. Incorporated in 1935, it is celebrating its 80th Anniversary in 2015. Without its presence and legacy, there probably would not have been the knowledge, resources and connections to start Co-opportunity.

"David Thompson's life is a Forest Gump-like journey through the co-op world. This book weaves through not only the story of Co-opportunity, but the food co-op and co-op movement in general. It's a treasure.**"**

Dan Nordley, Publisher, Cooperative Grocer and Past Director, Cooperative Grocer Information Network

"Then, in the late 1960s and 70s, the "new wave" of consumer co-ops began. Like its peers, Co-opportunity was born out of the ideas and philosophies of the 1960s, with a deep passion for equality, social justice, and to making whole foods available to its members. This set off a quiet revolution in what eventually became the "natural foods" industry.**"**

Karen Zimbelman, Director of Membership and Cooperative Relations, National Co+op™ Grocers

CHAPTER 4

THE SANTA MONICA CO-OP GROUP THAT FORMED CO-OPPORTUNITY

The young group of Santa Monica Co-op board members and activists would later form the core of Co-opportunity. The cast of co-op characters was:

Mike Timko, a long-time committed anarchist whose bible was Peter Kropotkin's book, "Mutual Aid." Mike was affiliated with the Santa Monica Co-op as the local agent for Mutual Service Insurance, then a cooperatively owned insurance company. Mike earned his living mostly by registering voters and working for the Peace and Freedom Party. He ran for Congress (CD26) in 1972, on the Peace and Freedom ticket and in 1974, for the State Board of Equalization. In both races, he gained about 4% of the vote. Mike was an inveterate letter writer to the LA Times and other Westside newspapers.

Mike lived in a converted motel in West LA just off Pico Boulevard, near the San Diego Freeway. He slept in the motel unit surrounded on two sides by Co-op books that he sold at public events. On the other side of his room were hundreds of neatly stacked five-gallon water containers. Annually, Mike took his vintage station wagon to Co-op Camp Sierra to fill up all his empty containers at the mountain water springs. He then returned with a year's supply of Co-op Camp water to LA. He drank nothing but that sacred water until the trip to Co-op Camp Sierra the next July. Mike was Co-opportunity's initial secretary and corporate record keeper.

George Tucker, who had a scientific background and had recently graduated from UCLA, where he was then working on computers. George was shy yet passionately committed to natural foods. He was also growing restless with the slow progress of changing the old Santa Monica Co-op product-by-product. As a result, he left the Santa Monica Co-op board and ran an herb-buying club out of his garage on Mississippi Avenue just around the corner from the Barrington

Co-op. George managed to spread his talents across all elements of the operational side.

And me, David Thompson. I was the anti-war, UFW and community organizer, public speaker and writer with ties to the English cooperative movement. I grabbed every piece of information I could about co-ops. Both my mother and father had worked for the Blackpool Industrial Co-operative Society at home in Blackpool, England. I lived in Santa Monica at 1325 ½ Princeton Street, above a garage filled with books about cooperatives. I was getting my Masters in Urban Planning at UCLA. On Princeton Street, I spent hours dreaming and writing about how co-ops could change the world. My role was to be the booster, believer and builder of Co-opportunity and the Cooperative Way.

By 1972, we had all regretfully left the Santa Monica Co-op Board, disappointed that the Co-op would close soon because it wouldn't change fast enough.

The three of us were then joined by Bill Lyfield, a long-time Venice activist and musician who was my first real-life model of cultural transformation. Bill was "Mr. Natural" and enjoyed exploring everything. At the time, he was living in George's house, Bill was on a spiritual journey that, thanks to his timely 'outbreaks' of calmness, aided us greatly during the many difficult times of birthing an organization.

Later, Bill returned totally to his mystical Jewish roots and became Eytan Ben Sheviya. Of the four founding members, Eytan worked the longest at the Co-op, where he ran the membership desk for a number of years. It was always a joy to come through Co-opportunity's doors and be greeted by Eytan's smiling face. I suspect that after George, Eytan was the first volunteer who became a paid employee. Eytan, born in 1927, passed away in October of 1991, at which time his life was celebrated by the many people who he touched along "The Way."

About that time, I was reading Martin Buber's book, "Paths in Utopia," up at Co-op Camp Sierra. It is one of the most impactful books on the different schools of cooperative philosophy and practice. Buber writes that he was most affected by his move to the young nation of Israel and the role of the kibbutz, moshav and cooperatives in building a utopian foundation for the new nation. One of Buber's points was that cooperatives had to have the ability to radically change to serve their new needs.

If only we could have succeeded in converting the Barrington Co-op! We would have had a 20,000 square foot store in West Los Angeles in 1972, featuring health foods. It would have been the largest health food co-op in the country. It would also have saved us 20 years of organizing and development and put us ahead in the natural foods industry. In 1972, there were only about ten "old wave" co-ops still in operation from the thousands that were set up in the 1930s. Of all the large "old wave" supermarket co-ops, only Hanover and Greenbelt would successfully make the leap from the "old wave" co-ops to the "new wave" ones. Scores of "old wave" co-ops died during the 1950-1970s. The younger generation was well aware that natural foods were the next major opportunity for food co-ops.

By 1973, we were meeting monthly in George's garage in West L.A. We sat uncomfortably on upturned milk crates with the garage door propped open. What a motley crew we must have seemed to anyone driving by. The only advantage appeared to be the fragrant aroma from the bags of herbs stored in the garage.

Our regular topic was, "How to start a natural foods co-op?" I would write leaflets, distribute them around UCLA, West Los Angeles, and Santa Monica. Then we would all wait for our 7 p.m. monthly membership meeting. Month-after-month, almost no one came. On occasion, a stranger turned up. Somehow we did gain a few members, collected a little bit of shared capital and kept the idea alive.

From the Santa Monica Co-op, we brought three important gifts: 1) An understanding and belief in the cooperative model, 2) A knowledge that, through Associated Cooperatives, the state wholesale, there was an economic and solidarity infrastructure that could support our interest in natural foods, and 3) Conferences and newsletters were available out there with new ideas, including one in particular emerging from Canada called a "Direct Charge Cooperative."

Finally, we agreed that no matter how many monthly meetings we held, the results would be the same. No one wanted to show up to help start the co-op by attending interminable meetings! We determined that we just had to go into business and the members would come - but how? How could we start the co-op, incorporate, and find the necessary start-up capital to begin? George stepped forward and said he was prepared to run the co-op alongside his herb business, form a limited partnership, rent a store and loan the co-op $5,000. A few of us also lent money. We all said we would invest and help in any way we could. That is how the Westside Buyers Club was formed which I believe was our original name.

"Starting a new co-op is a labor of love—it always was and always will be. Why else would a group of people with no grocery experience volunteer thousands of hours to open a new business? A business with a return on investment that Wall Street would scoff at? Because a food co-op provides its owners, workers, shoppers, and community with far more than financial speculation. Not only the obvious benefits of better food, better jobs, better support for the local economy, but also the expanding impact of cooperation can catalyze the revitalization of entire neighborhoods. Co-ops may or may not pay out cash dividends, but they always provide an amazing return in social capital.**"**

Stuart Reid, Executive Director, Food Co-op Initiative

"From countless meetings in a garage to a $25 million community owned business, the story of Co-opportunity, its roots in the Santa Monica Co-op and its local and national impact is an inspiration to communities everywhere. The tale is a community activist's must-read about committed and engaging characters who prevail over legal and financial obstacles and personality and political conflicts.**"**

Ann Hoyt, Cooperative Hall of Fame Inductee 2015, former Chair, National Cooperative Business Association, CCMA Superstar

CHAPTER 5
DIRECT CHARGE CO-OPS APPEAR IN CANADA & COME TO CALIFORNIA

This was the summer that the Direct Charge (DC) concept kicked in. Like other cooperators in California, news of the success of the Direct Charge method (details to follow) was spreading like wildfire among consumer cooperatives. The Direct Charge idea had been pioneered by Ralph Staples in Ontario, Canada, in the 1960s, and had been successfully applied. The concept had then moved quickly to Canada's eastern and western shores. The credit union leaders in Nanaimo on Vancouver Island, in British Columbia, adopted the idea and funded the opening of the first DC store in Western Canada in 1971.

The idea then jumped down to California, where it was taken up by co-op activists such as Morrie Lippman, a Palo Alto Co-op and AC board member and a former manager (in the early 1960s) of the Santa Monica Co-op. Morrie talked to the board at the Santa Monica Co-op about transferring to a Direct Charge as a way of saving the store, but the co-op leadership turned him down.

Morrie Lippman and his brother Ralph were co-op leaders from NYC. Ralph Lippman was manager of four union-sponsored housing cooperatives in NYC. Morrie had begun his co-op life on a cooperative farm in Michigan, described in the book "Quest of Heaven" (1957) by the founder Joseph J. Cohen. Morrie had come to California in the 1940s and had managed the Zone 26 Co-op, and then the Hollywood Co-op, and lastly the Santa Monica Co-op in the early1960s. He was the go-to-guy for consumer co-ops in Southern California.

After that, Morrie returned to NYC, where he managed the Chelsea Consumer Co-op located within the Penn South Housing Cooperative (where, among others, lived A. Philip Randolph, Bayard Rustin and other giants of the Civil Rights Movement). The March on Washington was mainly organized by the residents of the Penn South Co-op.

Later, Morrie founded the Consumer Cooperative Publishing Association and they funded the publication of a number of books about cooperatives. When Morrie returned this time to Northern California, he became once again a voice for cooperatives in the state on the boards of the Palo Alto Co-op, BriarPatch Menlo Park, Associated Cooperatives and Twin Pines Cooperative Foundation (then called BAND).

To see how some things run in the family, Ralph's son, David Lippman, was one of the early members of the Arcata Co-op. The Arcata Co-op then became North Coast Cooperatives. Later, David Lippman was appointed as the General Manager of North Coast Cooperatives and retired from that position in 2013. David also serves on the board of Associated Cooperatives and the Twin Pines Cooperative Foundation, as did his uncle Morrie Lippman. Even later, Morrie married Audrey Switzer, the mother of my wife, Ann Evans. So, coincidentally, Morrie became my step-father-in-law. But now back to the story.

The Palo Alto Co-op, while wishing to remain a conventional type of co-op store, wanted to see the development of newer and smaller-style co-ops. As a result, Palo Alto fostered the development and support of Direct Charge (DC) co-ops in California. In 1975, BriarPatch Cooperative Market in Menlo Park was the first one to replicate Nanaimo's DC method. When it reached its maximum of 500 active members, a second, yet independent, BriarPatch Co-op was started in nearby Mountain View in 1976. A third BriarPatch started in Grass Valley in 1978. What tied the new co-ops together was a cadre of "old wave" co-op leaders such as Morrie Lippman for Menlo Park and Harry Bailey (still volunteering at the co-op) for Grass Valley.

By the late 1970s, these other California co-ops were operating under the DC format: Co-opportunity, Isla Vista Food Co-op, Milpas Co-op (Santa Barbara), Santa Cruz Co-op, Santa Rosa Co-op, and the Venice-Ocean Park Co-op. Bob Burgess, one of the early Co-opportunity members, took the DC concept with him to Santa Barbara, and helped fit it into the Milpas Co-op. Bob, an engineer from UCLA, was the first Californian to set up charts to compare the effectiveness of the DC methods being used by the many co-ops.

George and I poured over materials about direct charge co-ops and, in particular, the literature sent to us from Nanaimo, and made numerous telephone calls to Rod Glen, President, and Hume Compton, Education Director of the Nanaimo Co-op (legally Mid Island Consumers' Cooperative), as well as to Morrie Lippman. George visited Nanaimo in 1973, and I followed in 1977, and then again later. The topic of the Direct Charge method filled the workshops at the California Cooperative Federation annual gatherings, as well as at AC's annual meetings. Many of us felt that DC was the way to go.

The idea of Direct Charge is both simple in structure, yet complicated by details. Direct Charge is a member-only format. The simple part was that every business had fixed costs (rent, lights, energy, insurance, interest, administration, etc.), which each co-op member had to pay their share of no matter whether they shopped or not. There were other costs called variable costs (labor, supplies) which were directly associated with each member's shopping trip.

What we also learned from Nanaimo was that consumers understood that it was more cost efficient for the store if it kept its opening hours limited, maintained a lower inventory and pushed through a lot of business when it was open so that its variable costs were controlled. The concept was that given each member was paying for the fixed costs whether or not they used the store, it was actually smarter to shop there as much as you could to reduce your fixed cost. The evidence was there from Nanaimo and the other direct charge cooperatives that the average shopping basket was much higher.

It is interesting that at this time the two fastest growing supermarket chains in Europe have replicated many of the frugal features of the DC model. Aldi and Lidl, both German supermarket chains, highlight limited selection, their own private label and, as a result, have high volume in smaller stores with fewer staff. Aldi Nord has owned Trader Joe's since 1979.

Nanaimo also taught us that the Direct Charge method could revolutionize capital acquisition. Because we were unsure of the reception for Direct Charge in California, we started with a modified program. For capital, we began with a more modest requirement of a one-time $25 investment with a $5 joining fee. We also started with a fifty-cent a week direct charge fee. We then added 5% to the cost of goods and 10% to perishables. We received our income equally from direct charge and mark-up. That was our economic plan. I remember thinking how long it took to get agreement on this set of share, fee and pricing policies.

I wrote in California Cooperative Leadership (January 1976): "What makes us possible is what makes Direct Charge co-ops a probability for many consumers.

1. We are a membership store not open to the public.
2. Members pay monthly fees whether they shop or not.
3. There are minimal capital costs.
4. We differ from traditional markets owing to differing wants: store size, types of inventory, opening hours, less need for centrally located sites.
5. An ability to move with the group.
6. Simple operational ability.
7. Recognizable savings on food bills.
8. A community or group solidarity based on the smaller scale.
9. Participation within the co-op.
10. A possibility for federation which allows for retention of immediate and philosophical power while sharing resources."

By late spring 1974, we found a vacant storefront on the West Side of Los Angeles at 11556 Santa Monica Boulevard. The store was on the south side of the street, between Federal and Butler Avenue. The store was only seven blocks from the old Co-op store on Barrington. The photo of the original store has my bicycle parked at the curb.

The storefront had all the right characteristics for a co-op, because, firstly, it didn't look like a store. It was small (less than 1,000 square feet), long and narrow. Its appearance was modest (some would say dull), had a high ceiling, windows only on the Santa Monica Boulevard side, front and back doors with five dedicated parking spots in the rear for delivery trucks and customers. Most importantly, its rent was cheap at $250 per month.

We obtained used equipment and shelving, a small produce cooler, an old cash register, and then stocked the place sky-high with products.

Some staff members seemed to spend their entire shift going up and down ladders. When done, the place looked like an out-of-control mini-warehouse. There were boxes everywhere and little room for people to pass in what could be generously called narrow aisles. The store opened on August 24, 1974, with little fanfare. Just as the Rochdale Pioneers of 1844, did 130 years earlier! Nevertheless, like them, we were nervous!

"If you take our current success for granted, David Thompson's chronicle of Co-opportunity's early years is a must-read. This is an inspirational memoir of a tremendously dedicated, visionary group of pioneers who realized a transformation and revolution in the retail food industry."

Michelle Jacobson, Co-opportunity Board Member (1989 – Present)

"Cooperators will be fascinated by how strongly this part history lesson, part memoir resonates with our own co-op stories, and appreciate that someone has taken the time to chronicle our shared experience in such detail and personal witness."

Dan Nordley, Publisher, Cooperative Grocer and Past Director, Cooperative Grocer Information Network

CHAPTER 6
HOW DID CO-OPPORTUNITY GET ITS NAME?

Santa Monica's Co-operative Natural Grocer

Shortly before opening the store, we were having one of our group meetings in a store front (borrowed with the help of Richard Katz – then my neighbor on Princeton, later Assembly Democratic Leader – for the evening from the Westside Democratic Club) on Santa Monica Boulevard in West Los Angeles. We kept the door open because of the intense summer heat.

During the time we were discussing what to name our co-op, a young, bearded hippie came in and sat by the open door. He had no shoes on and no one to this day remembers his name, because we never asked him and he never gave it. We earnestly and passionately all had favorite names for this co-op that was to change the world. The intense discussion went on for quite a while with little sense that we would or could reach agreement.

The young man sat there quietly listening to our discussion of what to name the co-op before asking if he might speak.

We all turned around to look at this compete stranger, who said, "I hope you don't mind, but I've been listening to you talk about this as a great opportunity and how it's a co-op - Why not call it: Co-opportunity?"

We all stared at his young, bearded, idealistic face and were stunned by his simple suggestion. There was a lengthy silence from those of us who had been thinking a long time about our name. Then there was a slow nodding of heads. As organizers, we probably all thought it was our right to choose the name for our organization. After all we had been thinking about our name for months.

Wrong, this guy had coined a name that immediately had the right ring to it. We had held our breath for so long some of us were turning blue. Oh, my god, that would be our name. Out of the silence, someone motioned to adopt Co-opportunity as our name, all those in favor? The vote was unanimous.

We all turned to thank the stranger, but by then he had walked out into the cooler night air and was gone forever. Yet, this stranger with no name had given us ours.

How similar we were to the Rochdale Pioneers, who started their own store on December 21, 1844. On opening day, they were 28 weaving families; we were twenty members. We started by opening three-days-a-week, as did they. We started with all volunteers, so did they. The Rochdale Co-op opened with five items for sale. In that area, we had them beat, with probably 100 items for sale. The Rochdale Pioneers opened in the middle of winter and wondered in that weather who might come through the door. We opened in the middle of summer and wondered who would come to a dark store in the summer heat.

Wondering and worrying were two things we shared with the Rochdale Pioneers. Yet at the same time, we shared our hopes and aspirations, and our desire to change the marketplace with better food and better business practices. While we felt lonely, we did not feel alone. We had the knowledge that history and the Rochdale Pioneers were on our side. We knew that natural foods had a future and that cooperation was the method that would best serve consumers.

"For over 30 years, David Thompson has been my eyes and ears to the world of cooperatives. His account of Co-opportunity's beginnings and achievements reinforces my appreciation of the contribution of coops in the area of my greatest passions, from democratic governance to ecological farming and food. Thanks, Co-opportunity, for your contribution to a better world. Happy 40th Anniversary. **"**

Frances Moore Lappé, Co-Founder Small Planet Institute and author of 18 books, including, "Diet for a Small Planet," and "EcoMind."

"Successful co-ops like Co-opportunity, now celebrating their 40th anniversary, know that sound business practices are as essential to success as are a commitment to people and environment, and that strong membership support, sufficient capital, ability to adapt to changes in the marketplace, and an openness to finding more ways to work together are all critical to our success -- as individual co-ops and as a united cooperative sector. **"**

Robynn Shrader, CEO, National Co+op™ Grocers

CHAPTER 7

THE OLD SANTA MONICA CO-OP DIES AS WE ARE BEING BORN

In January 1975, only months after we opened, the Santa Monica Co-op's store closed its doors forever. A page in the Berkeley Co-op News had one article on our opening and in the same issue another article on the Santa Monica Co-op closing. For nearly 40 years, the Santa Monica Co-op had been an outpost for the consumer voice and cooperative model in Los Angeles. We were sad to see such an ending to the dreams of a previous generation. It was one of the saddest events of my co-op life.

Co-opportunity now had to bear the responsibility of representing the ideal and practice of cooperation in Southern California. We never felt competitive with the old Santa Monica Co-op, as by the time they closed, they were still doing over $40,000 a week, and we were not yet doing $4,000 a week. We had tried to change the old co-op and had failed. It was now even more incumbent upon us to make the DC model work. We did benefit, however, from knowing that co-ops worked thanks to our experience as board members. We also gained a number of loyal Santa Monica Co-op members and through Fernando Sendejas, the old co-op generously gave us many of their fixtures and equipment. We were a Phoenix rising from the ashes.

Co-opportunity began with $5,000 in capital and 20 paid up members. Two months later, we had 100 members, with operating losses of about $200 per month. Store hours were 1.30 p.m. to 6.30 p.m., Thursday through Saturday. Initially, the members did all the work as volunteers. By spring of 1975, we were doing enough business to hire George Tucker and Jan Schipper as co-managers, each being paid $440 per month. Every person working at the store got $2.30 per hour.

By then, we had also changed the opening hours to 1.30 p.m. to 7. 30 p.m. on Thursdays and Fridays, and noon to 6.30 p.m. on Saturdays. We changed the direct charge fee to $3, $5 for a couple and $1 for each additional person. For each hour a member worked at the store, they could get a one-dollar reduction in their direct charge. Non-member shoppers were initially charged 10 percent, and later 20 percent, over member prices. Non-member shopping was discontinued when we moved to the Broadway store in Santa Monica.

We had begun Co-opportunity with the monthly meetings in George's garage. At first, anyone who showed up at the monthly meetings and was a member got to vote on all the issues. When the store opened, we began to call the group the co-ordinating committee. Later, we began to meet monthly at Jan Schipper's apartment near the Safeway in West Los Angeles. On good days, we met on her balcony and in the winter we met inside. The co-ordinating committee met for many months regarding reviewing and making endless policy changes.

Owing to our growth and the newness of the DC model, we struggled to keep up with the fast changes and to retain equity in our policies. With the DC method, you have to consider the way it impacts different sized households, contributions of capital, and pricing, as well as the appropriate ratio between fixed and operating costs.

We would constantly review the Nanaimo material to see how they did it, as if it were a Canadian Co-operative Bible. One of the other issues we worried about was that the Nanaimo model was members only. We felt we couldn't do that until we reached a certain volume. We thought it wrong to have an empty store and then tell someone they could not shop. We needed those shoppers, those lookers, and those curious ones. We eventually agreed that we would close off membership at the present store at 500 active households.

With its health food orientation, Co-opportunity grew quickly. From the original 20 households in August 1974, the membership grew to 400 households by September 1975. (As of that month, members had provided $12,575 in share capital, and the loans due had been reduced to $1,000). A monthly sales volume of $7,000 was straining the store's capacity. Therefore, the steering committee began to search for a larger location.

Given our growth, we decided to change the capital structure to help prepare us for the move to another store. By September of 1975, we voted to raise the "fair share" limit from $25 to $100, by asking every member to pay an additional $5 per month. Prior to and during the re-location, Co-opportunity took a few personal loans from members of the core group at 9 percent simple interest. As of July 31, 1976, loans outstanding totaled $5,545, while member shares outstanding stood at $27,269.

By then, individuals like Tina Handy and Gail Suber had joined the staff and they brought great people skills and energy. Tina recounts that, "We were one of the few places to get natural foods and specialized products." As a result, during the early years, Co-opportunity was a real community. People were very friendly and the staff was quite tight-knit. Tina remembers that later the bulletin board at the Broadway location in Santa Monica was a real connection point for people. "It was a place to find a commune, get a cross-country ride, or find a vegetarian household."

"Once the only place to find natural and organic foods, co-ops today compete in increasingly competitive markets that challenge our relevance. Successful co-ops like Co-opportunity, now celebrating their 40th anniversary, know that sound business practices are as essential to success as are a commitment to people and environment, and that strong membership support, sufficient capital, ability to adapt to changes in the marketplace, and an openness to finding more ways to work together are all critical to our success – as individual co-ops and as a united cooperative sector. **"**

Robynn Shrader, CEO, National Co+op™ Grocers

CHAPTER 8
FINDING BROADWAY

Finding a new storefront for Co-opportunity was a task delegated to me. After much deliberation of sites and plotting out where the membership lived, we decided that our first choice for a location would be in Santa Monica. The main reason for the choice was our desire to have Co-opportunity feel like part of a specific community and thus have immediate local impact. Santa Monica, with its defined city limits, its own City Council and smaller population (then 80,000, seemed a more livable city than Los Angeles. Our purpose fell in line with the recently adopted Seventh Co-op Principal, Concern for Community.

I wasted no time setting off on a lengthy pilgrimage to find our new store, driving round and round Santa Monica and West Los Angeles. All the existing grocery store sites, however, were taken. From there, I began searching for any empty store about 3,000 square feet that could be transformed into a grocery store. There were a few, but the rental and outfitting costs put them far beyond our reach. My green VW bug (called Connolly after the Irish Independence Leader) was beginning to run on empty. Whenever I found anything within our budget, it was always in an industrial area. Viable locations were almost non-existent. In an act of tired desperation, I actually strongly recommended a site near Bundy under the Santa Monica Freeway.

Then one day in Santa Monica, I saw a "For Sale" sign at 15th and Broadway - a quiet, commercial-industrial area. It was on a lot packed with Hertz rental trucks and used cars. I called the number with trepidation. An impatient voice answered, "Yes!"

"I'd like to talk to you about the property at 15th and Broadway." He replied curtly, "Can you come over right away?"

Minutes later, in an office a few blocks away, I was meeting Fred Plotke for the first time. He whisked me into an office piled with papers, and told me to sit down while hurriedly answering another phone call.

"OK," he said, mincing no words, "tell me what you want, who you are and when you can move in?"

And so the negotiations began. He told me what he wanted per square foot, which, in comparison to other offers, was reasonable. Yet, I grimaced. At my age, it seemed unreasonable to charge someone rent for doing good. We went on to discuss other details. I told him I had to take his offer back to the board. We stood up, shook hands and I left his office in disbelief that we actually might have a site. Within days, I made the presentation to the Board and we all went down to look at the site. The Board was anxious to move - but very definitely not under the Santa Monica Freeway. Within a few weeks it was a done deal and we had a lease very favorable to Co-opportunity.

So why was Fred Plotke so willing to lease to us? By most standards, we were a bunch of hippies whose goal was to change the world, selling strange food, and negotiating for the rent deposit, which we couldn't pay just then. The answer was: Plotke had a commitment from a bank to finance the construction of the building, but only when it was fully leased. Leasing to us would close the deal. The building had five bays in it of 1500 feet each, and we would take the last two.

With a lease in hand for the remaining two bays, Plotke would be off to the bank. Plotke was, therefore, very willing to work with the unique limitations of a young, growing cooperative enterprise. Because of the bays being built to suit, we were able to work with Plotke to design where the utilities, pipes, toilets, doors and storage would go. Although it was a sparse utilitarian building, it quite suited our purposes. Whenever we had a problem with something, he was willing to let it go and find another solution. He needed us as much as we needed him and, thus, our two interests had common ground.

Apparently, I arrived at the right time, when his needs were as critical as ours. How the stars lined up! Thank you forever, Mr. Plotke, for giving us a hand when we needed it most. About 30 years later, I wanted to track Mr. Plotke down to thank him. He was still working out of the same office. I called him up and arranged to meet with him. I thanked him for giving us our start. His personality had not changed. He said, "Thank you," gruffly, then smiled, and our meeting was over just as quickly as the first meeting had been.

On July 4, 1976, after a nine-month search, the co-op moved from its first store at 11556 Santa Monica Boulevard into the newly built 3,000 square-foot store 1.5 miles away at 1530 Broadway in Santa Monica. The building had been designed for the co-op's needs. It was a fitting day to move, as we used member's cars, vans and trucks to move all the inventory and fixtures down Santa Monica Boulevard in a caravan that continued into the night.

Co-opportunity was gaining its independence on that very July 4th evening that the City of Santa Monica had spent thousands of dollars on fireworks to celebrate, or so it seemed, our move to their fair city. It was kind of exciting to see the magnificent fireworks over Santa Monica Bay as we drove all our belongings to the new store. Once installed, our 500 member families responded positively to the new location's modern interior, layout, and the spaciousness of the new building. Co-opportunity received extremely good media coverage regarding the move, and business grew quickly.

The author writing at 1325 Princeton St., Santa Monica. (Photo by Faren Bachelis)

Co-opportunity storefront at 11665 Santa Monica Blvd in West Los Angeles. (Photo by Philip Clayton-Thompson)

The author looking in the window of the West LA Co-opportunity store, c. 1974. (Photo by Philip Clayton-Thompson)

Co-opportunity in West Los Angeles (store interior).

Packaging station at West LA Store (1970s).

Sign on door of West LA store. "Closed on July 5th. We've moved to 1530 Broadway."

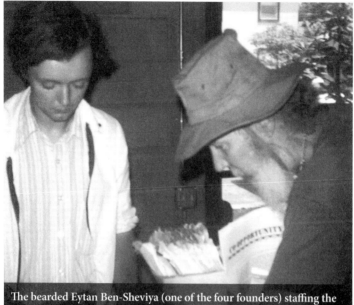

The bearded Eytan Ben-Sheviya (one of the four founders) staffing the membership desk at the new store at 1530 Broadway, Santa Monica.

Fundraiser for Co-opportunity at author's rear apartment at 1325 Princeton in Santa Monica.

Calling the "For Sale" number on this sign led the author to Fred Plotke and the second location of Co-opportunity.

1530 Broadway site being cleared for construction of the new store. Author's green VW Bug, "Connolly," in background.

Later Co-opportunity sign on 1530 Broadway, fostered by the beloved Will Simon.

Some of the first members to shop at 1530 Broadway, Santa Monica.

Grand Opening 1530 Broadway.

Membership Meeting sign-in Co-opportunity, 1980s.

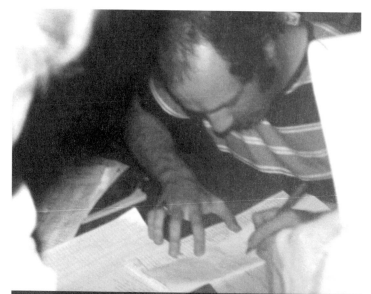

Peter Fonda-Bonardi doing check off at a Co-opportunity membership meeting (1970s).

Member Meeting in shell of new store at Broadway, Roberta Mahoney (early member left) and Gail Suber (early staff member right).

Bruce Palma, now manager, working at the store at 1530 Broadway.

Will Simon working in warehouse at Co-opportunity store 1530 Broadway.

The well-loved mural at 1530 Broadway.

Upton Sinclair, populist author and candidate for Governor of California in 1934. Sinclair's platform to End Poverty in California (EPIC) emphasized cooperatives as a way out of the Depression.

CO - OP
By
UPTON SINCLAIR

The cover of the book entitled "Co-op" by Upton Sinclair.

Jerry Voorhis, President Emeritus of the National Cooperative Business Association (formerly Cooperative League of the USA), giving a talk in Santa Monica. In the 1970s-80s, Jerry attended many events sponsored by Co-opportunity and other Westside cooperatives.

Derek Shearer, early Co-opportunity board member in 1970s. Derek was later appointed to the Board of the National Cooperative Bank by President Carter.

Robert Neptune, Manager Associated Cooperatives

Robert Neptune, longtime General Manager of Associated Cooperatives, Inc. Main supplier to Co-opportunity in its early days.

CALIFORNIA'S UNCOMMON MARKETS
THE STORY OF THE CONSUMERS COOPERATIVES 1935-1971
BY ROBERT NEPTUNE

Robert Neptune's book, "California's Uncommon Markets" about the history of consumer cooperatives in California.

On left, Morrie Lippman, longtime California Co-op Leader (GM of Consumers Cooperative Society of Santa Monica in the 1970s, longtime AC Board member and advocate of Direct Charge Co-ops).

Sheila and Michael Bernard staffing the offices of the Southern California Cooperating Warehouse (1970s).

Ruth Yanatta and James Conn at Grand Opening of new store at 1530 Broadway, Santa Monica.

New Co-opportunity sign at 1530 Broadway, Santa Monica.

The store of the old Santa Monica Co-op at 2021 S. Barrington in West Los Angeles. Standing outside the store are early Co-opportunity members Joan Gosewich and Ira Galperin. Their daughter, Jill Quanstrom, later became the Marketing Manager for Skagit Valley Co-op in Mount Vernon, Washington. The old Santa Monica Co-op closed in 1975 after almost 40 years of being in business on the Westside.

The trucks of Associated Cooperative delivered goods to Co-opportunity.

Author in a workshop at Co-op Camp Sierra, early 1980s.

Co-opportunity Today, 2015, at 1525 Broadway.

"Co-ops like Co-opportunity have built resilient and vibrant businesses, and their successful practices and accumulated knowledge need to be leveraged! Together, we can realize our vision of more co-ops, benefiting more people, in more communities. We are stronger together!**"**

Robynn Shrader, CEO, National Co+op™ Grocers

"There are over 120 more (food co-ops) that are organizing right now. Why the renewed interest? I believe it is in large part due to the impact that "New Wave" co-ops like Co-opportunity have had on the people who experience the power of cooperation first-hand. In our mobile society, families often relocate and when they leave a co-op behind, its absence leaves an empty space in their lives that inspires them to start a food co-op in their new community.**"**

Stuart Reid, Executive Director, Food Co-op Initiative

CHAPTER 9

CO-OPPORTUNITY OPENS ON BROADWAY

To celebrate our Grand Opening, we planned a daylong set of activities. We began with ribbon-cutting ceremonies and speeches by local celebrities such as, Ruth Goldway (formerly Yannatta) and the Reverend James Conn of the Church in Ocean Beach. Thanks, too, to Denny Zane, Ed Pearl, Derek Shearer and others.

Once the store was officially opened, we had a great puppet show in the parking lot, which attracted hundreds of members and their kids. Of course, everyone had to park somewhere else. Then for the rest of the day, many local musicians gave a community concert. As the sun went down over our lovely new store, we all felt proud of being in our new location in our adopted community. With the turnout we had that day and the response to our larger, cleaner, attractive store, we knew we had made the right decision. The street lights turned on and softly illuminated our beautiful new Co-opportunity sign. The Co-op's sign incorporated the rainbow as the symbol of international cooperation. All in all, it was a great first night on Broadway.

By December 1976, member households had risen to 800, and volume was averaging $20,000 per week. With tongue in cheek, we named the newsletter "Long Lines." In anticipation of this growth, the co-op had incorporated in January 1976, and changed its status from a limited partnership to a cooperative corporation in July 1976. Co-opportunity elected its first board of directors in September 1976. .

TAKING OVER THE NEXT BAY

In February 1977, an opportunity arose to obtain an additional 1,500-square-foot bay adjacent to the Co-op's two bays. Although there was cautious resistance to leasing the additional space, the board and workers saw its potential and worked out a plan whereby

700 square feet was leased in March, and the remaining 800 square feet later in September 1977.

In March of 1977, I wrote the following notes after a meeting in the new space:

"It was a room full of cardboard boxes delivered from Associated Cooperatives. We were there to plan for the additional space and the space that would open up in the existing store. On the dusty floor, around a blue print of the building, were workers and active co-op members."

"Tina Handy and Gail Suber from the staff were animatedly talking of their needs as workers. Gregor, our Polish refugee architect member, was looking for design solutions. Good old Al Fractor added his own wisdom from years of experience. John Sels was a little out of it, having worked on the Co-op truck's blown engine all day. Over in the corner, Megan Rossiter and I were measuring the wall to see where a door could connect the two spaces."

"All of us were excited about how the store would change. Even better was the group interaction, building together, helping each other, discussing, and working it through with each other. 'It's these moments that make the Co-op a real thing for me.'"

LEARNING IN THE LOFT

While building the new addition, we wondered how to provide space for meetings. Ruth Goldway wrote, "I remember our Co-op board meetings were held in the back half of the store. We sat on the most uncomfortable folding chairs and I was always cold because we were in the food storage area where things had to be kept cool."

With ground floor retail at a premium, we came up with the idea of building a loft above the cold storage coolers. A couple of our members who were carpenters built the contraption. You got there by climbing a ladder and then sat under the wide strips of silver-backed insulation and the unfinished roof. There were no windows; it was very warm in the summer and underneath you could hear deliveries being stacked and staff talking.

The co-op's meetings looked like a get-together of the Weather Underground. There was a dim light, second-hand chairs, a pile of old carpets to lean against, but no table. Yet, for us, who climbed that ladder once a month to attend the board meetings, it was the heart and mind of Co-opportunity. It was where we planned for the future and where we made the changes we needed to make. Through the addition, the Board now had a place of its own in which to meet.

For those who love cooperative folklore, Co-opportunity is a shining example of history repeating itself. In 1846, a couple of years after renting their first store, the Rochdale Pioneers were able to rent the floor above their store. The Pioneers used the upstairs space for their board meetings, education classes and a library. The upstairs was converted from a warehouse into their member education center. Although now a cooperative museum, the upper floors at the museum in Rochdale remain a place for cooperative education.

Co-opportunity was no different. People by the dozens ended up yearning to learn in the loft. In that humble space, we did our then mandatory member orientation programs, and held our staff training and education classes. In between events, the loft was the worker's break room, lunchroom and a special place to nap.

Marianne Rolston, an active co-op member who became Chair of the Education Committee, was intent on impacting people. While Marianne held that position, she kept the loft lively with activity and climbed those stairs more than any other volunteer. Co-ops are fortunate when people like Marianne come along to ensure that a certain focus and competency exist to really make a difference. In those days, we were much more invested in educating people about what a co-op was and why it was a different form of corporation.

"S erving on the board of Co-opportunity provided me with my first chance to help guide a business enterprise, albeit one with a social, as well as a commercial purpose. Working with David Thompson, Ruth Goldway and others, I played a small part in helping Co-opportunity to deal with internal strife and smooth out its management operation so that it could survive and prosper.**"**

Ambassador Derek Shearer Chevalier Professor of Diplomacy; Director, McKinnon Center for Global Affairs, Occidental College

CHAPTER 10
CRACKS APPEAR IN OUR CO-OP

The Co-op, however, did not successfully execute its plan for the store addition. The major organizational changes and the sudden jump in size from 1,000 square feet in July 1976, to 3,700 square feet in March 1977, went beyond the Co-op's management capacity to maintain control over its operations.

Co-opportunity also added a produce wholesale to its operations in 1977. The wholesale created additional needs for capital and inventory, yet operated with a separate team and lack of oversight and control. An attempt to finance the fast growth through a bank loan ended when our bank, the Ocean Park Bank, refused to lend Co-opportunity money. Co-opportunity was their fastest growing customer, but personal guarantees were the bank's policy. (Happily, that bank turndown led to Co-opportunity playing a major role in creating the National Consumer Cooperative Bank).

In September 1977, the board also agreed with George to a major increase in staff wages without specifying where the additional monies were to come from. Beginning in July 1977, the co-op experienced a downturn in profits, which was clearly not just a summer slump. The problem lay in three areas we failed to keep our eyes on: (1) the additional space had not been utilized as quickly as it should have been, (2) Co-opportunity had set a limit on how many active members there would be, and (3) we had increased labor costs without assuring income.

Most importantly, however, we discovered too late that we had made major errors in counting active members. This had prevented the co-op from allowing members in from the waiting list, (the co-op had room for at least 100 more households and over 200 households were on the waiting list). This problem brought about a large drop in volume that further escalated losses. An average household spent approximately $25 per week: 100 x $25 = $2,500 in sales volume per week. The new member fees would also have added an additional

$500 in new capital per month, in addition to the initial $2,500 from the new members' first month's share payment (100 x $25). Sadly, the co-op was slow to react to the problem, and months went by without ameliorating the problem, as the losses increased.

Not only were Co-opportunity's problems operational but organizational as well. Initially, the membership group had acted as a collective: any member turning up could vote on whatever was on the agenda that evening. Then when the two co-managers (Tucker and Schipper) were hired, the membership group acted as a sort of advisory team to them. Structurally, Co-opportunity was the name above the door, however, the business inside was still a limited partnership owned by George Tucker.

Because of state regulations, we were not able to incorporate as a cooperative corporation until January 6, 1976, at which point the new Board took on more responsibility for the organization, its assets, selling of shares and monitoring of management, etc. In July of 1976, we transferred the business from a limited partnership to a cooperative corporation.

As soon as we showed proof we were incorporated as a cooperative, we were allowed to join Associated Cooperatives as a cost plus member. When Co-opportunity was incorporated, the Charter Board of Directors began to exercise authority for the organization. To follow the bylaws, we then held elections for the Board of Directors in September of 1976.

Unfortunately, the incredible expansion of the business, a period of puzzling losses, and the Board's growing role placed tremendous stress upon the organization. In particular, we did not have a-priori mechanism for clearly separating the Co-op from George Tucker's limited partnership business. Consequently, what we thought of as a co-op was technically a $2,000,000 private business. At the same time as negotiating the transfer, George also sat on the Board of Directors. Thus, there were built-in conflicts of interest, which we could no longer ignore. Neither side had prepared for the moment when the co-op would replace the limited partnership.

As soon as the board started to act as stewards for the business, other differences escalated and tension over the control and direction of the organization grew on both sides. Soon, the new Board and George realized that their differences were insurmountable and on a tremendous collision course. We agreed that the governance and direction of the co-op needed to be decided by a membership meeting.

The entire membership was notified by mail of a Special Membership Meeting being called during the spring of 1977. I asked Derek Shearer, a lecturer at the UCLA School of Architecture and Urban Planning and a respected writer and co-op member, to chair the meeting. To make sure we had a fair meeting process, we hired the Parliamentarian from the Santa Monica League of Women Voters to be present to advise. The meeting was held at a large church in Santa Monica on either Santa Monica or Wilshire Boulevard. Nearly 500 members turned up for the meeting. There was an air of foreboding as we quietly filed into the church.

It was the darkest night in Co-opportunity's young history. Both sides presented their case and scores of members and staff spoke. After every voice was heard, the members voted on the set of prepared motions sent out in the mail. At the end of the evening, the membership voted to support the direction outlined by the Board to fully act as a cooperative under the stewardship of the elected board. We all walked away from the church saddened that we had not found any other way to solve the situation. The board was authorized to change the locks on the store and assume corporate, legal and financial responsibility.

By the next day, George was gone and we had to hastily fill the management gap. People like Gail Suber and Tina Handy and others took turns providing management leadership. Without George as manager and with a new board consumed in the running of the business, there was an absence of an operational power center. For quite a while, the Co-op ran without truly having a manager. Later, the workers suggested to the board that we should use the opportunity to experiment with worker self-management. The board reluctantly accepted the offer, figuring that the organization could not tolerate any more pressure.

With my ties at the School of Architecture and Urban Planning at UCLA, I asked the UCLA Graduate School of Management to have a team of graduate students analyze Co-opportunity's business. By fall of 1977, the board and workers accepted the offer of technical assistance. A UCLA team led by Svetlana de Kansky and Benjamin Darche then took an outsider's view of our business and operational and organizational structure.

The UCLA team did an immediate review and arrived at two main topics for study, 1) Board-Management relations and structure, and 2) Pricing, margin and fee policy. For the first topic, the team taught the board to differentiate policy setting from policy implementation. With a weak organizational structure, the board was totally micro-managing the operation. As a result, the managers and staff were very frustrated and antagonistic to the board. One of the other main policy questions was: "What type of co-op were we going to be? One for low cost food or one which was purely natural foods and organic produce?"

Regarding the second topic, the team suggested alternatives to everyone having to work. They proposed that we encourage everyone to do a work shift, however for those who didn't, they could choose to pay a higher monthly fee.

When presented in full, the UCLA report was sobering and simple – we needed to change our ways quickly or there would be no co-op. Fortunately, the Co-op agreed to act on each segment as it was completed.

After a special membership meeting in fall of 1977, the board: (1) raised the direct charge as of January 1, 1978, to $3.50 per adult, (2) allowed member work credit at $1.75 per hour, (3) revised membership accounting practices and expanded membership, and (4) encouraged the staff to reduce wages as a percentage of sales to approximately 10 percent. (They had risen from 6.7 percent in March 1977, to 11.5 percent by October 1977).

During 1978, the Co-op began to stabilize. With the help of the UCLA team, the staff created a management system that provided closer control and supervision of the operation. The board and staff agreed upon their areas of influence and that substantially reduced points of conflict. Volume grew again as the membership was expanded.

As the Co-op grew, it realized that it needed also to comply with the existing state regulations regulating the issue and sales of securities. Co-opportunity applied for a securities permit. Fortunately, the Co-op's changed fiscal situation allowed it to withstand financially the 13-month wait during which it was not allowed to sell membership shares. Co-opportunity had its first profitable year in 1979, five years after its inception.

By 1980, the Co-op's average monthly retail volume was over $150,000. There were 1,200 active households with more than a hundred on the waiting list. The staff was comprised of over 20 full-time workers and a number of part-timers, plus a growing number of members working off their direct charge. As the Co-op renewed its sale of shares, it gave priority to a $2,500 loan to help other community members establish the Venice-Ocean Park Co-op. At the store level, we purchased a number of major pieces of equipment, including three new computerized cash registers. The 1980 retail and wholesale volume moved Co-opportunity beyond the $2 million mark.

"Co-opportunity and co-ops across the country pioneered in offering cleaner food and still lead their communities in education about our food supply. They do this while modeling democracy in action through cooperative enterprise: providing high-quality goods and expanding services, modeling transparent policies and governance, and keeping more capital in the local community while facilitating broader ownership.**"**

Dave Gutknecht, Editor, Cooperative Grocer

CHAPTER 11
WHERE DOES MONEY COME FROM?

MEMBERSHIPS AND SHARE CAPITAL

On joining Co-opportunity, there was a non-refundable membership fee of $5 to cover the costs of entry and exit. Members were asked to purchase one $25 share and pay in an additional $5 per month until each member has paid $100 in total share capital. Paid in share capital totaled $135,523 as of July 31, 1980, although accumulated operational losses had reduced total member equity to $89,422.

LOAN CAPITAL

Co-opportunity used member loans from some of us to get off the ground initially, and to partially finance its move to a new store until the fall of 1977. After that, adequate capital was available from the membership shares and store operation and Co-opportunity stopped using member loans as a source of capital.

NET SAVING

During the first four years of operation, Co-opportunity had difficulty controlling its rapid growth, with its operating expenses being greater than its income. (Actually this may have been a plus from the merchandising viewpoint. When chains open new supermarkets, they expect them to lose money during the first few years until they attract enough customers to raise sales volume to levels where the store can operate efficiently and profitably.) In the start-up period, losses were made up from the surplus created through the sale of member shares. A lot of our capital was tied up in the constantly increasing inventory.

With a higher sales volume, however, a stronger management component, and a pause in growth, the Co-op witnessed its first profitable year in fiscal 1979. Unfortunately, in 1980 to early 1981, Co-opportunity again suffered operating losses, owing in part, to major losses in its produce wholesale.

The shelf margin then provided over two-thirds of the retail gross margin, with direct charge providing less than one-third. The board had agreed that the direct charge should equal the fixed operating expenses of the store, while the shelf margin should equal the variable expenses. Over the following years, Co-opportunity slowly dropped the DC method and the work requirement. Like many other co-ops in competitive markets, Co-opportunity needed to change to meet the differing needs of its members and the lifestyle patterns that changed from the 1970s to the 1990s.

CO-OP WHOLESALE

Although Co-opportunity went into business in 1974, it would be two years before we could join Associated Cooperatives in order to use its warehouse in Richmond, California. At the start, we were not ordering enough to use AC even as a non-member. By 1976, we were ordering $1,800 of goods every three weeks. After becoming an incorporated cooperative in 1976, we were thus able to join AC. During that time, we needed to build our business enough to benefit from regular shipments from Northern California. Once we started using AC, we came into wonderful contacts with all the other start-up natural food co-ops in California. AC put us in touch with scores of other new co-ops facing the same questions about the natural foods industry and growth.

Soon after opening, we joined the Southern California Cooperating Community, a small regional warehouse, which was supplying hundreds of buying clubs with organic produce and natural foods. Michael and Sheila Bernard are to be credited for their unselfish commitment to growing the new wholesale, and for the SCCC published, must-read zealous newsletter: Raisin Consciousness.

Soon, Co-opportunity became SCCC's biggest single customer. To obtain our conventional produce, we rented a truck once a week to pick up from the downtown Central Produce Market. Much of the rest of our products were delivered by small natural food businesses to our back door.

CALIFORNIA CO-OP CONFERENCE AND THE CALIFORNIA COOPERATIVE FEDERATION

At the conclusion of the CLUSA conference in San Francisco in 1974, the Palo Alto Co-op hosted a one-day gathering later named the First Annual California Co-op Conference. This conference brought the "new wave" of co-ops together for the first time, with many topics discussed. There was excitement in the air and an agreement was reached to hold an annual conference for food co-ops, particularly to connect the "new wave" of food co-ops.

No one from Southern California participated in the first California Co-op Conference. At the second, held in Santa Cruz in 1975, I was asked to be the keynote speaker about the Rochdale Pioneers and Co-op Capital, as well as to lead a workshop on co-op literature and direct charge co-ops.

It was at this conference that I first met Ann M. Evans, one of the co-founders of the Davis Food Co-op. In 1979, we would be married. The Isla Vista and Santa Barbara Co-ops and SCCC were the other Southern California attendees. The next conference was held in 1976, in Santa Barbara, where we had a very strong Southern California co-op, with 200 attendees. The annual conference subsequently moved around to a different location each year.

From these activities rose the need to have a statewide organization capable of running the conference and providing a continued voice for cooperatives throughout the year. At a meeting of "new wave" co-op leaders under the pine trees at Co-op Camp Sierra, we formed the California Cooperative Federation (CCF). The CCF performed a lively networking service for the natural food co-ops for over a decade.

❝I am very proud that I was on the board and part of the early years of Co-opportunity, and I recognize how the store helped me in my later efforts to build farmers markets in Santa Monica when I was that city's mayor. Co-opportunity is now an established, well-respected retail leader. Thank you, David, for writing this history of how remarkably successful people can be when working together for the common good.**❞**

Ruth Goldway, Former Co-opportunity Board Member and former Mayor of Santa Monica

CHAPTER 12
BUILDING COMMUNITY, COOPERATIVES AND THE FARMERS MARKET

When Co-opportunity moved to the Santa Monica store, we began to focus more on how to build community. We had not done events at the old store, owing to the fact we were so busy and did not really have a location that favored community activities.

Later on, the annual meetings were generally held as a picnic gathering for a number of years at Marina Park. Interviewed by Ginny Winn in 1988, Eytan Ben Sheviya said, "At one annual meeting we had something like 400-500 people. But that was exceptional. At the big meetings, it was something like 200. We had picnics where a 100 or more showed up and then we had other events with very few. A lot of it depended on what time of year, how much it cost, how much advance publicity there was, how many volunteers were active, that sort of thing." Most often the Annual Meetings were held at the Unitarian Church in Santa Monica. The Minister, Reverend Ernie Pipes, was very visible in the community on anti-war and civil rights activities, so we all felt very much at home in that church.

For a number of years, Co-opportunity organized "Rochdale Night" at the Santa Monica Unitarian Church, commemorating the opening of the Rochdale Pioneers' store on December 21, 1844. In conjunction with the celebration, we held a Holiday Crafts Fair. Our best Rochdale Night occurred when the Los Angeles Farmworker Chorale did a community sing-along ending with an ear-shattering rendition of the farm worker anthem "De Colores." The event was free and ended with a community potluck. At our first fair in 1976, 50 people attended, by 1978, there were 150 people attending. In the December newsletter, we urged people to buy their holiday gifts from non-commercial sources or at the Holiday Crafts Sale.

I wrote in the Alternative Celebrations Catalog of 1978, "As we developed the tradition of Rochdale Night and the Crafts Fair, we hoped to guide our member's money into support for a more human and just lifestyle. We have the light of the Rochdale Pioneers to keep us to the path. Our cooperatives can unite in this celebration to bring change, development and liberation."

All of these activities took a great deal of organizing by the staff and committees, followed by the much-needed, immense support of member volunteers. Without the commitment of these folk, Co-opportunity would not have been able to make a contribution to building community among our members.

COOPERATIVE HOUSING

Co-opportunity fostered the Westside Housing Group with the intent to create cooperative housing as an adjunct to Co-opportunity, and as an example of cooperation among co-operatives. We looked at converting apartment buildings into cooperatives, but capacity and capital were sorely lacking. An offshoot of the idea did pan out when a small group of people, including a number of Co-opportunity members, collectively bought an apartment building in Santa Monica. The Westside Housing Group met for a couple of years at the Unitarian Church, but ran out of steam, owing to the high costs of land in Santa Monica and the lack of financing for cooperatives.

Later on, we worked with co-op consultant, Ed Kirshner, who was brought in by the Santa Monica Council to look at how to bring cooperatives into a rent controlled environment. As a result, City policy gave certain priorities to limited equity cooperatives, and, as a result, there have been a couple of conversions. When the Santa Monica Housing Corporation (SMHC) was set up to provide a range of affordable housing, including cooperatives, there was less of a need for the Westside Housing Group. Fortunately, many of the initial staff of the SMHC were members of Co-opportunity and had previously done cooperative housing, which undoubtedly contributed to seeing some cooperative and shared housing developed in Santa Monica, Venice and Ocean Beach.

STARTING THE SANTA MONICA FARMERS MARKET

While Ruth Goldway was on the Co-op board (approximately 1976-78), and prior to her election to the Santa Monica Council (1979-83), she became interested in opening a Farmers Market in Santa Monica. Ruth was then Assistant Director of Consumer Affairs in the Jerry Brown Administration. By 1977, Ruth was the lead person in Consumer Affairs on California's Farmers Markets.

At the time, I served as a representative of the food co-ops on the Public Advisory Board for the State Board of Food and Agriculture. Richard Rominger, the State Director, who later became the USDA Deputy Secretary of Agriculture, was a strong supporter of organic farming and farmers markets. He asked George Hellyer, who was on his staff, to get a farmers market going in Santa Monica. Because Co-opportunity was the natural home to start one, we agreed to sponsor the Farmers Market organizer, manage the contract and I offered to supervise his work.

Steven Ogawa was the young organizer. It was his first job out of college and he was thrown into an urban environment with the many conflicting political agendas. Nonetheless, Ruth was very determined to make the farmers market happen, and Co-opportunity gave Steven plenty of access to sources in the LA area. It took one year longer than we thought to get prepared, owing to a serious insurance gap that Co-opportunity agreed to cover. We started the work in spring of 1977, with the Farmers Market scheduled to open in summer 1978. Unfortunately, Co-opportunity's insurance solution was still not satisfactory to the City, and the resistance remained strong, with the City Council unwilling to allow the Farmers Market to go forward. Undaunted, we started all over again.

Ruth Yanatta recounts, "As my first act on the Council in 1979, I got the City to close Arizona Avenue on Wednesdays and got someone in the City Manager's office to work with the LA-based Certified Farmers Market staff to set up a weekly market. The old-line conservatives in Santa Monica complained that the Farmers Market was socialism. We wondered how free markets could be called socialism and they said it was because we were closing the street. That market was so successful that a Saturday market was initiated within about a year. Ida Bucher, who ran the First Presbyterian Nursery School, was our Poster Queen for the first promotions. She was the beloved, white haired fairy godmother type who the conservative establishment didn't dare to criticize. Today, the Santa Monica Farmers Market is one of the most visited in the state and has become a major tourist attraction in the city. This August of 2015, I visited the Wednesday Santa Monica Farmers Market once again. What a great experience that Co-opportunity helped to create.

ORGANIC FARMING, DIRECT MARKETING AND ALTERNATIVE AGRICULTURE

Along with the other natural food co-ops in California, Co-opportunity helped to create a market for organic produce. The more consumers buy, the higher the demand, with more small farmers increasing their organic production. The legislation establishing Farmers Markets began at the Federal level in 1975, with strong support from the Co-operative League of the USA, and food cooperatives. The initial direct marketing legislation had only one California Congress member as co-sponsor, former Vice President of Associated Cooperatives and UCLA student co-op leader and now deceased Congressman George Brown.

A pilot program followed in 1975, in California, concluding with the passage of state regulations in 1979. The roll out of these changes created tremendous opportunities for organic production. At the statewide Co-op meetings, there were always many organic farming devotees holding workshops on the direct marketing that should be between the farmer and the consumer.

A group of co-op activists led by Don Rothenberg, the Education Director at the Berkeley Co-op, Ann Evans of the Davis Food Co-op, Mark Lipson with the Santa Cruz Co-op, and Ruth Yanatta and I at Co-opportunity were the main co-op links in supporting the regulations establishing Farmers Markets, Direct Marketing and Organic certification.

Ann Evans was then also managing the Co-op Development Program of the Department of Consumers Affairs under Governor Brown. Ann had co-founded the Davis Food Co-op, which went on to sponsor the creation of the Davis Farmers Market. With that experience, Ann became the point person on alternative food production and distribution for the State of California.

Through the effort of hundreds of co-op activists and others around California, the State's Department of Food and Agriculture under its Director, Richard Rominger, adopted regulations for Direct Marketing on April 29, 1979.

"The intent of this Article is to facilitate the transfer of food from producers directly to consumers while maintaining sufficient regulatory control to ensure that the food transferred is of acceptable quality and that the transfers are conducted honestly and fairly." With that rather mundane wording, an era of alternative marketing began in California, led by the creation of Farmers Markets that have blossomed throughout the state.

"One of the things that happened was with Ruth Yanatta-Goldway, who was Mayor of Santa Monica at one time, was on the Board," said Eytan in his 1988 interview with Ginny Winn. "Her profession had been as consumer-advocate. As a member of the Board, she spearheaded a move, with others around the state, to get a law to define 'organic' in reference to food and growing food. We had no control up to this time. Because there was no law governing it, people could call something organic and get away with it and charge more money. They would be speaking technically of something being organic material, not in the sense of it being grown without pesticides and so on. The Co-op was partly instrumental in getting the law passed. Our members signed a big petition. We had both a committee and the Board lobbying. It was really very exciting, one of my dreams come true."

During that time, the Board of Co-opportunity supported many legislative initiatives on bills which changed the food policy of the State of California. Many of the things we take for granted today were actually against the law at that time. Not only did we speak out on these issues, but we at Co-opportunity were also the best source for ballot signatures in Southern California.

SAVE-A-TREE BAG

Co-opportunity was one of the first customers of a company that was just starting in Los Angeles. Richard Katz's parents asked me to meet with a young idealist, who wanted to promote re-usable canvas bags to help save the world. The young man was Kim Marienthal and he was in his 20s. Kim had been awakened and impacted by the first Earth Day in 1970. His was the first company to market re-usable shopping bags.

Kim had a simple concept: grocery stores should sell reusable canvas bags as a way of getting their customers to reduce their usage of paper or plastic bags. Kim had founded his business after locating a US maker of natural canvas shopping bags. The Save-A-Tree logo was imprinted on one side and the store's logo could be imprinted on the other.

In 2014, doing the research for the book, I tracked Kim down. He now lives in the East Bay. He ran the company for many years, but recently turned the company over to his sister. The Save-A-Tree bag is still helping to save the earth and still being sold in hundreds of shops around the country. Kim remembers our meetings and the fact that Co-opportunity was not only the first co-op to buy his bag, but one of his first customers. When he got Co-opportunity's relatively large order Kim knew that his business would succeed.

PUBLIC POLICY

Through Associated Cooperatives, Fight Inflation Together (FIT), the Oil Crisis, UFW and other groups Co-opportunity played an important role in offering alternatives to the status quo. We did that in a number of ways: we supported the regulations allowing farmers markets, the development of organic standards and certain food boycotts. As a representative of Associated Cooperatives and California's food co-ops at a State Senate hearing in Sacramento, I spoke in favor of the original Bottle Bill. The original concept was for consumers to be given a rebate when they returned bottles to the store.

All the other food retailers said, "No bottles in our backrooms." Food co-ops were the only retailers in California willing to take back the bottles at the store. The good news was that the bill passed and California took up recycling. The bad news was that the large grocery chains amended the bill and the state adopted a redemption rather than a return system.

ALTERNATIVE ECONOMICS

The 1970s were the heyday for many efforts to establish alternative economics and business. For many of the proponents in California, Co-opportunity was pointed to as a good example of community ownership and responsiveness. Leaders of Co-opportunity were often featured at conferences held by groups such as the National and State Conference on Alternative Public Policy.

A group of Co-opportunity's leaders were associated with the School of Architecture and Urban Planning at UCLA, as well as with Tom Hayden's Campaign for Economic Democracy. CED had a similar populist stance to Upton Sinclair's EPIC campaign and historians saw a lot of similarities between the two men's campaigns for Governor. Most of the leadership of CED joined Co-opportunity, including Tom Hayden and Jane Fonda, Ruth Goldway and Derek Shearer, Reverend Jim Conn from the Ocean Park Church and Denny Zane.

Three of those early members, Ruth Goldway, Jim Conn and Denny Zane, were elected to the Santa Monica Council and all became Mayors of Santa Monica. When Ruth Goldway announced her candidacy for the State Assembly in 1978, she held her press conference in front of Co-opportunity to show her commitment to consumer issues and alternative policies.

CALIFORNIA CO-OP POLICY

Selling of Shares. Like most other food co-ops in California during the 1970s, Co-opportunity broke the law when it sold shares to get started. None of us knew this at the time. We copied the articles and bylaws of the Santa Monica Consumers Cooperative, which sold shares to the public. Somewhere along the way, however, we discovered that the State of California had a legal process for a cooperative corporation to issue shares and we were not following it.

At that time, co-ops were required to go through a costly legal effort to gain a permit to sell shares. California law required a cooperative corporation to first obtain a permit before having the right to sell shares to the public. Amongst other requirements, a co-op had to place $50,000 in escrow before the Department of Corporations would allow it to open for business. Conforming to that would have made going into business impossible. Every dollar we raised we needed to use immediately.

Having understood the requirements and being aware of our exposure, I requested that AC work on crafting a legislative solution. Robert (Bob) Neptune, the General Manager of AC, and myself were appointed to take the lead in getting the securities requirements changed for consumer co-ops.

Fortunately, the Chair of the key committee in the California Assembly was John T. Knox. He was the member representing Richmond (where AC had its HQ) and played a major role in corporate law. Bob and I met with Assembly Member Knox on a number of occasions in Sacramento, and also with the Department of Corporations. While we were hoping for a wider exemption, we were able to arrive at an Assembly Bill that allowed consumer cooperatives to collect up to $100 of share investment that was exempt from regulation.

It took two years of effort, but finally, a new co-op bill was signed into law that allowed cooperatives incorporated under the Consumer Cooperative Law to gather shares up to $100 from each member without having to file a securities permit. The passage of the law meant that all the new food cooperatives were now lawful in their share programs. Years later, I lobbied again for an amendment to the law and the maximum was moved up to $300, where it still stands today. On August 12, 2015, Governor Brown signed into law a measure that now allows consumer co–ops to obtain up to $1,000 without a permit. We've come a long way on the road to capital.

"My practical experience with Co-opportunity in Santa Monica gave me ideas and information which I put to good use when President Carter appointed me to the founding board of the National Cooperative Bank in Washington, D.C. Working with David Thompson on a national level, I helped to populate the top management of the bank with talented co-op entrepreneurs and managers from around the country.**"**

Ambassador Derek Shearer Chevalier Professor of Diplomacy; Director, McKinnon Center for Global Affairs, Occidental College

CHAPTER 13
YOU'RE KIDDING! YOU PEOPLE WANT A LOAN?

With Co-opportunity growing at such a rapid pace, our need for long-term working capital outstripped the member investments in shares. We approached the Small Business Administration, but found out that because the SBA regards co-operatives as non-profits, we were ineligible borrowers. At a meeting in Boston, I attended in August of 2015, I learned that our four-decade-long effort to get SBA approval of consumer cooperatives was about a year away from being approved.

Because we needed credit badly, we met with a loan officer at the Ocean Park Bank. Since we banked there, we felt they would understand us. We showed them our growth, documented our success and thought that things were going well. "We'd love to make you a loan," the bank manager said. "Here are the forms, fill them out and bring them back." We shook hands and left.

We didn't read the forms until we got back to the store. Everything was fine except for the last part. The Bank required that the board members had to agree jointly and severally to co-sign the loan. If the co-op could not pay the loan back then the board members would be held liable for the loan. None of us had any assets and neither were any of us willing to sign the papers. We explained that to the Ocean Park Bank and we never did get the loan. Soon thereafter, Co-opportunity joined in the national efforts to form a National Cooperative Bank.

NATIONAL CONSUMER COOPERATIVE BANK

The idea of a National Consumer Cooperative Bank took flight at the national meeting of the Cooperative League of the USA held in San Francisco in 1974. Soon after, I was asked to co-chair the California efforts along with Don Rothenberg, Education Director for the Berkeley Co-op. Don and I had worked together on Tom Bradley's first campaign for Mayor of Los Angeles in 1982. At every

Co-op Bank Hearing we attended and in every letter I wrote about it, I recounted Co-opportunity's turndown by the Ocean Park Bank, and the need for this thriving new cooperative sector to have a bank of its own. The testimony I wrote for Congress about Co-opportunity was actually taken by one of the Catholic orders and inserted into the permanent record of the Senate Banking Committee's hearings. Work on the National Consumer Cooperative Bank (NCCB) Act began in 1974, and continued until the legislation passed in 1978.

One Co-opportunity member, who played an important role in gaining passage of the Bank Act, was Derek Shearer. Derek was a writer who covered alternative economics and had close ties to Senator Cranston and Ralph Nader. Derek believed strongly in the idea of the Co-op Bank, and wrote about it in numerous statewide and national publications.

We also had great help from Jerry Voorhis, who also wanted to help his friends in Santa Monica. Another supporter was Congressman George Brown Jr., one of the founders of the student housing co-op at UCLA, and a former Vice-President of Associated Cooperatives. Owing to his strong co-op ties, I arranged for George Brown Jr. to give a speech at Santa Monica College when he ran in 1970 for the US Senate on an anti-war platform.

Co-opportunity became the headquarters in Southern California for passing the Co-op Bank legislation, as did the Berkeley Co-op for Northern California. At Co-opportunity, we engineered a massive letter writing campaign and petition drive that impacted many members of the Southern California congressional delegation. Once the Bank was established, Co-opportunity actively supported the efforts of Alan Cranston and Ralph Nader to have Derek Shearer appointed to the charter board of the Bank. Derek served on the National Consumer Cooperative Bank Board for two terms and later was appointed by President Clinton to be US Ambassador to Finland.

A major disappointment for me and for Co-opportunity Manager, Will Simon, was that although we worked so hard to establish the Bank, Co-opportunity had not yet been able to borrow from it. On the other hand, NCCB did make a small loan to VOP, which kept it afloat when it ran into cash flow difficulties in its early stages.

JAM TODAY

At that 1974 California Co-op Conference, one group stepped forward to offer to put out a quarterly publication as a tool of education and communication among the "new wave" co-ops. It was called "Jam Today," after a term from "Alice in Wonderland." Operated by a team shepherded by Ann Evans, a founder of the Davis Food Co-op, "Jam Today" was the delightful purveyor of news and SKU's (Stock Keeping Units) about the natural foods co-op scene in California. If you want to know what people were thinking back then, "Jam Today" captured the essence of a generation when natural foods was part of a new way to build a new society and a peaceful path to a real revolution. Co-opportunity was an immediate subscriber to and supporter of "Jam Today," which was published by a collective from 1974, until it gracefully retired in the 1980s.

CO-OP CAMP SIERRA

Thanks to the old Santa Monica Co-op's participation in AC, a number of people from Southern California participated in the annual trek to Co-op Camp Sierra. The tradition continued as Co-opportunity took on the mantle of co-op leadership in the South. A number of the Co-opportunity stalwarts became regular camp participants, such as Mike Timko, Gail Suber, Tina Handy, her mother Rosemary, Rosemary's husband, Joe Schwartz, and myself. Even though there was now no store, a number of the old Santa Monica Co-op members still made the journey to Co-op Camp Sierra.

At Co-op Camp, and especially during the education sessions, we learned about the world of cooperatives. It was there at the camp that we learned of the victory for the National Consumer Cooperative Bank by one vote in the House, and where we formed the California

Cooperative Federation. Somehow our little co-op immersed in selling groceries was linked to this worldwide effort to build a better world. It helped to lessen the burden of our everyday concern, it helped us to look up and dream rather than look down and worry. As the week went by, we filled up our tank with great Co-op energy; we found new friends, discovered new solutions and went down the mountain empowered to fight for another year.

"David Thompson's loving history of Co-opportunity reflects the often messy, sometimes frustrating, and always rewarding process of starting and nurturing, a new food co-op. Every one of the beautiful and vibrant co-ops we enjoy today (and often take for granted) started with the hard work, commitment and dreams of a small group of people. Their efforts inspire a new generation of co-op organizers as a "third wave" of food co-ops washes across the U.S. "

Stuart Reid, Executive Director, Food Co-op Initiative

CHAPTER 14

HELPING TO START THE VENICE OCEAN PARK CO-OPERATIVE COMMONWEALTH

About 1977, and in keeping with the idea of growing the cooperative idea, I initiated the idea of Co-opportunity opening another store in the Venice Ocean Park area. I had proposed to the board that Co-opportunity adopt a long-range plan to eventually have five neighborhood stores on the Westside. After much discussion at the board level it was decided, however, that we supported the idea of other co-op stores in the area but not as branches of or to have branches of Co-opportunity.

It was the religion of food cooperatives in that era that each co-op should have only one store and that if people wanted a co-op, they had to build it themselves. I tried my best to explain to the board how long and hard it had taken us to get Co-opportunity off the ground and how much easier it would be to develop other locations that could also give us economies of scale. These were the days of "Small is Beautiful," however, and there was no appetite for additional locations.

So, once again I committed myself to sitting in empty rooms for a couple of years while we waited for a bolt of lightning to hit. I gathered a group of co-op supporters in Venice Ocean Park (VOP), and thanks to the generosity of Reverend James Conn, we began to meet monthly at the Church in Ocean Park.

Unfortunately, the only room available for us to use was the children's nursery in the basement. The only thing worse than sitting on upturned milk cartons for two years is to perch carefully (not sit) on bright yellow plastic children's chairs for two years while trying to write on avocado green children's tables. How could anyone entering the nursery for the first time have taken us seriously? Well, in fact, no one did.

Just as with Co-opportunity, what helped was getting the word out in the community. People knew something was going on. A co-op was being planned. Other than that, though, hardly anyone paid attention to our distribution of thousands of flyers all over the area or our notices in the paper and church bulletins.

Just as the old Santa Monica Co-op impacted the founders of Co-opportunity, now, so, too, did some members of Co-opportunity, who were strengthened by Co-opportunity as a model, knew what we were trying to do. Slowly, we gathered names, collected capital and got the word out. I was still serving on the board of Co-opportunity and the organization did everything it could to help the new co-op get started. Ben Kogan, another Co-opportunity Director, also served on both boards as a commitment to cooperation among cooperatives. Co-opportunity did mailings for us to its members in Venice Ocean Park, allowed us to make announcements at meetings, to leaflet outside the store and to put stories in the newsletter. Co-opportunity also committed that once we got started, it would help with staff support, transportation, buying together and sharing shipments. Finally, it made the most important gesture of all - a matching grant of $2,500 towards opening the doors. Immediately, we obtained a similar commitment through the Church of $2,500 from the Methodist Ministry of Los Angeles and then later $6,000 in pledges from the 80 members we had when the store opened.

This time, Kurt Buser, a committed Swiss born graduate student at the School of Architecture and Urban Planning, stepped forward to take the lead. Kurt found a location for VOP at 839 Lincoln Blvd. We put a deposit down, got a lot of equipment from the Southern California Cooperating Community and help from Co-opportunity. VOP opened on August 1979. It began with a management collective structure that included Lillian Gilbreth (daughter of the "Cheaper by the Dozen" Family), Michael Bernard and Jim Congdon, with Ross Moster as the first official manager in 1981. Regretfully, Jim Congdon drowned in a freak accident in Santa Monica Bay. Great help with the organizing came from Peter and Claudia Fonda-Bernardi and his brother Mario. Their house was VOP's house for a few years.

Once again a co-op started with little inventory, used equipment and irrepressible hope. Without that match from Co-opportunity providing the yeast for other funds, it's doubtful that VOP would ever have gotten off the ground. Fortunately, VOP also had a committed group of people, and one of them, Ross Moster, who dedicated over two decades of his life to keeping the co-op store going, mostly as general manager, and sometimes also as a board member. Ross eventually emigrated to Canada. He lives in Vancouver now, and still supports an alternative culture.

Later, Kurt Buser served on the board of Amazing Grains in Nebraska. Later still, Kurt served on the board of the Ashland Food Co-op in Ashland, Oregon. It was fun in about 2003, to have a meal with Kurt in downtown Ashland. He and I were happy that we were still building a better world and were both still in cooperatives.

"Co-opportunity, like its peers and many co-ops to come, has learned to leverage its cooperative ownership structure to bring economic power to the people. The impact has been enormous – both in its local community, as well as throughout the country. Here's to many more years of consumer empowerment and continued growth of a strong and vibrant cooperative sector – in Santa Monica and beyond.**"**

Karen Zimbelman, Director of Membership and Cooperative Relations, National Co+op™ Grocers

"In "Co-opportunity: The Rise of a Community Owned Market," Thompson describes himself and others as earnest and committed, people who didn't set out to make history, but their determination to contribute has left a unique legacy. These are important, poignant, well-written stories that contribute to a powerful understanding of the motivations and accomplishments of the American food co-op movement.**"**

Patricia Cumbie, author of "Growing with Purpose, Forty Years of Seward Community Cooperative"

"But this revolution is not over. Co-opportunity and its members can continue to lead the movement for GMO labeling, food security and ensuring that concern for people is a value of those in the food industry. Thank you, David, for nurturing Co-opportunity through its early years, writing this book and inspiring me to work for our cooperative future.**"**

Michelle Jacobson, Co-opportunity Board Member (1989 – Present), Past President (2002-2004), Past Twin Pines Cooperative Foundation Board Member and now Howard Bowers Fund Trustee

CHAPTER 15
CONCLUDING THE BEGINNING YEARS

In spring 1979, I got into my green VW, drove one last time to Co-opportunity as an active member, purchased my supplies for the trip north to Davis, California, to court Ann Evans. We married in September of 1980. I've been active in the Davis Food Co-op (DFC) ever since. I served 17 years on the board of the DFC, making me their longest-ever serving board member.

I was sad, however, that I would no longer be part of the daily life of the co-op store I loved. Especially when it seemed to be emerging from its lowest point. There would still be a number of growing years for the organization and once again some very difficult ones, including years fighting to overcome bankruptcy. "Thank you," I always say to Co-opportunity's former General Manager, Will Simon. The lessons I learned from him, I took with me to Davis. The Davis Food Co-op went through similar growth pains about five years later.

Fortunately, Co-opportunity's board took the brave step of hiring Will Simon and giving him real power as a manager. Will had the enviable task of plugging a hundred holes in a sinking organization before it could move forward again. Under a succession of active and constructive boards, and with Will at the helm, Co-opportunity weathered a stormy period in the 1980s to emerge as a healthy organization in the 1990s, well prepared for the next century. The story of that important era has been written in Chapter 16 by Bruce Palma, who after Will's retirement, took the helm of GM. Building upon what Will had started, Bruce has taken Co-opportunity from strength-to-strength. Congratulations to him and his team for positioning Co-opportunity for the opportunities ahead.

Today, Co-opportunity occupies an attractive building. It is clean and shiny inside and its operations are the envy of the natural foods industry. In thinking about Co-opportunity today, Ruth Goldway states, "The organic food chains and other niche segments of the food industry owe their existence to you and others in the Co-op movement."

The story of Co-opportunity tells you that getting to here from there was no easy course. Were it not for brave and dedicated members, management and staff, our cooperative would not exist. The early years and the commitment of ordinary people should not be forgotten. The efforts of the hundreds of pioneers have ensured that a consumer cooperative has served the people of Santa Monica since 1935.

In retrospect, the story of Co-opportunity's beginnings seem hardly different than what Upton Sinclair described on the cover of "Co-op" published in 1936: "A story of the self-help cooperatives, in which a thousand men (and women) and their families combine to win independence. They toil, argue, starve and suffer, hope and fear, love and hate, there is humor, pathos, excitement, tragedy, courage and wisdom in their lives." We had all of those elements in the founding of Co-opportunity.

The City of Santa Monica and the present members of Co-opportunity should be proud of their rich past and excited about their future. Co-opportunity is a natural foods retailer ready for this new Millennium. Yet Co-opportunity is more than that; it is a cooperative organization owned by its members and serving the community. Its profits are distributed to its members living on Main Street, Santa Monica. None of the profits from Co-opportunity ever leave to go to Wall Street to pay off unknown international investors.

Through the seven cooperative principles, Co-opportunity shares those people-based principles with over one billion people in every corner of the world. Perhaps the Seventh Principle says it best, "Concern for Community." That has been the enduring goal of Co-opportunity since it began and thankfully still is.

I was proud to be present in Manchester, England, in 1995, to be one of the ten US delegates to the International Cooperative Alliance to vote for the "Co-operative Principles for the 21st Century." Born in nearby Blackpool, I was part of the historical world of the Rochdale Pioneers, and despite having co-founded Co-opportunity and living in Northern California, I remain a representative of the new world.

Author's Note: This history is only one co-founder's recollections of what transpired over 40 years ago. With the passing of time and people, it is likely that my own memory of certain events and times is not 100% accurate. I apologize for any errors or omissions. If readers spot needed corrections or have additional anecdotes that they feel should be added to this history, please send them to Co-opportunity.

"Having become over the years deeply reliant on Will Simon's operational stewardship, Co-opportunity was forced to grow up when he retired. That transition point could have doomed the Co-op, as it has for a number of other co-ops. As a Board, we labored over the process of General Manager succession, but ultimately landed on an "insider" with the promotion of Bruce Palma.

Our instincts proved right, as Bruce has led a steady march of professionalizing our management structure. Bruce and his management team have created systems that prodded staff to higher productivity and more accountability. They have done that with a keen ear to keeping the unique community and atmosphere that defines the Co-op difference.**"**

Jens B. Koepke, Co-opportunity Board Member (2000-present) and Past President, Board Member, Twin Pines Cooperative Foundation.

"Thank you, David, for documenting the history of Co-opportunity and their 40 years of service. And congratulations to Bruce and the Board on reaching this impressive milestone. From all of us at North Coast Co-op, a hearty welcome to the 40 year club!**"**

David Lippman, Former General Manager, North Coast Cooperative & Board Member, Twin Pines Cooperative Foundation

CHAPTER 16
AFTERWORD AND THE FUTURE
RECOLLECTIONS OF THE WILL SIMON
YEARS (1986-2006)
by Bruce Palma
(Employee since 1985. General Manager, 2006 – present.)

In 2013, I videotaped a series of interviews with Will Simon, general manager from 1986 – 2006. In them, he recounted his history and experience working at Co-opportunity. The following narrative draws heavily from those interviews.

A NEW SHERIFF IN TOWN

Before becoming Co-opportunity's general manager in 1986, Will Simon had owned and managed several natural foods stores in the 1960s and 1970s. When he applied for the job at Co-opportunity, he had been unemployed. He placed an ad in the Los Angeles Times and got a call the same night from Lois Arkin, Executive Director of the nonprofit CRSP (the Cooperative Resources & Services Project) Institute for Urban Ecovillages. She told him there was a little co-op in Santa Monica that was in bankruptcy. She asked him if he could help them out. Will thought, "I don't think so, I don't want to fight another battle." So he declined. Three or four days later he answered a blind ad in the local paper. He called the number and it turned out to be Co-opportunity. He figured he might as well interview for the position. He went to the store a few days later, looked around and thought, "I hope they don't hire me, this place is terrible…" The interview was held in the wooden, hand-made loft above the small office in the warehouse. Will said he purposefully gave a terrible interview. He didn't want the job. He said no to most questions. Several days later he got a call from Robin Wales, the Board President. Robin said they wanted to hire him. Will still didn't want the job but his wife said he'd better find something and get out of the house and make some money. So Wilbur Simon became the new general manager of Co-opportunity in 1986.

His first day on the job was the following Monday. It was a cold, rainy morning. He was told to ask for a tall person named Paul. When Will got to the back door, he knocked and the door was answered by a tall person. But it wasn't Paul. It was someone else. And this person wouldn't let Will in. Will said, "I'm the new general manager." He still wouldn't let Will in. Will said, "I don't know who you are, but as soon as I get in, I'm going to fire you." He was finally let in and the first thing he saw was a banner hung on the wall that read: "Welcome Will Simon." The board had a party over the weekend celebrating Will's hiring, but hadn't invited him.

So, on Will's first day the store opened and customers and employees started coming in to work and shop. Will was still trying to find his way around when he got a phone call. It was from a board member. The board member said, "What are you doing there?" Will said he was working. The board member said, "No, you're not hired. The full board didn't vote. You have to leave." Will was happy to leave. He didn't want the job in the first place. He was walking out the door when he got another call from the same board member. He was told to disregard the last call, it was a mistake. He was actually hired.

So Will was hired, fired and re-hired his first day on the job.

According to Will, this was not good. He went home that night and told his wife he didn't want to work there. She said, "Just give it a chance." He went back the next day and started finding his way around. Again, he got a call from yet another board member. The board member said he had gotten a call from someone claiming Will was selling commercial watermelon but calling it organic. Will had no idea what they were talking about. He went to the produce department and found one single large watermelon in a wooden bin under a case. There was no sign on the bin. Will didn't know if it was commercial, organic or from Mars. He called the board member back and said, "This is ridiculous, there's one melon with no sign on the bin." Will thinks it was most likely the previous general manager who had called the board member.

THE STORE OR LACK THEREOF

The store condition was so bad Will immediately wondered if he had made the right decision. Then he thought, "It's just a job. I'll probably only be here about three months before it's shut down."

His first impressions were bad. "The store was ugly. It was an ugly little store. It looked awful." There was very little product on the shelves and no real retail merchandising. The previous management didn't really understand what customers wanted. There was a county health closure notice on the front door. The sign said if things weren't cleaned up, the store would close within five to ten days. The concrete floor inside was painted green, but the paint was peeling, so patches of concrete flooring showed throughout the store. There was a stack of empty boxes in the front of the store clogging the entrance. One of the refrigerated juice cases could barely get colder than 50 degrees. Worst of all, for an organic natural foods store, the produce department was in terrible shape. There were two very dirty refrigerated produce cases and dirty wooden shelving and displays filled with dead, limpid produce. Will thought, "It's no wonder people won't buy it."

The store layout consisted of two sections: the front—registers, customer service and membership desk, a few old refrigerated cases, produce section, grocery shelving—then there was a ramp leading down to the back of the store, which had a second room for the bulk section. This was also the entrance to the tiny warehouse, even smaller office (enough for two desks) and the wooden loft built above the office. Upstairs in the loft there was a carpeted room with a couch. This was where board meetings were held, and eventually two tiny offices were created. It was definitely like being in a tree house. The wooden stairs creaked when you walked on them, and the floor creaked as well.

After the watermelon incident, Will realized the first step was giving the produce department a complete makeover. None of the existing produce staff had any professional experience. Will knew he had to find someone who could turn the department around. He called a few people he knew and eventually hired Richie Roeckl as produce manager. Richie had been a produce wholesaler and had worked for grocery chains. He was an experienced produce man and a classic "green grocer" character. He had that engaging "in your face" personality that helped sell produce.

Immediately after Ritchie was hired, Will closed the produce department for a weekend and cleaned house. He and Richie worked the entire weekend, throwing out every piece of produce in the store. They brought out all the wooden produce bins and shelving into the tiny parking lot, hand cleaned them all, scrubbing off all the dirt and grime. An entire inventory of fresh produce was ordered, a local handyman re-arranged the displays, and the produce was merchandised beautifully.

The produce department had been doing roughly $200 a day in sales before the makeover. When the new department was unveiled on the following Monday, the department did $700 in sales—a 250 percent increase overnight. It was that quick.

"If you build it, they will come…"

The same thing happened throughout the store. Sales increased immediately after proper merchandising and more products were displayed to create a sense of abundance. As Will put it, "People said, 'Oh there's stuff we can buy…'"

But it wasn't quite that easy. In order to stock more products, cash was needed, and there was barely enough cash in the bank to buy a box of organic watermelons. Deliveries were all COD (Cash on Delivery), which didn't help a struggling business with little or no cash. So, for the first few weeks, Will did what he could. He had a friend who owned one of the major natural foods distribution companies in Southern California, Nature's Best. Will was able to secure 60 days credit on all product purchases. That's how he got product in the store to fill the shelves and create a sense of abundance. Sales grew with every positive change. More sales meant more cash flow. Once product started arriving, Will merchandised as best as he could. He moved stuff from back to front. He created appealing displays. One of the hot categories back then was bottled juices. So Will moved juices closer to the front of the store.

There was no vitamin and body care department, just some shelving with a few supplement bottles. He hired Robin Enwright, vitamin and body care manager at One Life, a natural foods store on the border of Santa Monica and Venice. Robin had a lot of product knowledge and vitamin retailing experience. After filling and merchandising the section with product, customers responded immediately. After that, it was easier to grow the member and customer base and increase sales.

Another key change was made. When Will took over, non-members paid a 15% surcharge on top of the shelf price. Co-op members paid the shelf price. This system was designed to entice non-members to become members, and increase the membership base. On the one hand, the strategy helped create new members, but on the other, it also created a negative impression of the co-op for non-members. Will knew he only had about three months to turn the store around, so decisions were made quickly. He eliminated the surcharge system. Non-members would pay shelf price. But he also added a member discount system, and gave all members a 10% discount on all products. Will remembers this change really helped the store grow sales and customer counts. Members still had a benefit and non-members weren't alienated. They were also incentivized to become members.

Will's welcome from most members and shoppers wasn't exactly warm and fuzzy. Many members and customers were angry at him for making changes. Some would say, "I don't like the way the store is now. I like the way it was!" He would say, "You mean bankrupt?" He let them know the co-op would've probably been closed in the next few months. His first annual meeting wasn't any easier. People were really angry at him for coming in and changing the status quo. It got so contentious that at one point Eytan Ben Sheviya, one of the four founding members, had to stand up and defend Will. Eytan was one of Will's co-op mentors and allies.

Will's first experience of Eytan was watching Eytan play percussion through the store. Eytan was a professional Latin percussionist and loved to hand out his instruments to staff and customers on the sales floor and start an impromptu jam session. Since he was trying to change the culture from a wild free-for-all, to a professional grocery store, he wanted to ask Eytan to stop playing percussion on the sales floor. It took will awhile, but he finally asked Eytan to refrain from playing percussion in the store. Eytan agreed. He also became a key mentor to Will. Eytan and Will would meet afternoons in the old wooden loft in the warehouse. Eytan taught Will about Co-opportunity's history, the co-op movement, co-op principles and the cooperative spirit. Will said his meetings and conversations with Eytan turned him into a "believer." At first he didn't even want the job; then he figured he'd spend a few months trying to save the place. After a while, as Will began to understand the co-operative mission and co-operative principles and values, it became a truly worthwhile cause, not just a job.

Will did what any successful retailer did to increase sales and customers—he studied their shopping patterns, assessed their needs, created a welcoming, pleasant shopping environment and gave them the products they wanted. Most of the store's equipment didn't work well and needed to be replaced. The two ancient cash registers the store had were constantly breaking down. Not having much cash on hand, Will found some used registers that worked much better. He replaced some refrigerated cases and made other changes on the sales floor. Over the course of the first year people really noticed the changes and sales grew rapidly.

Before Will was hired, the store's staff had very little business experience. No one working there at the time knew how to properly markup products from cost to get an acceptable amount of "gross margin" which was needed to cover expenses and create a year-end profit. The philosophy was that profit wasn't good. There was even a sign on the front of the store that read, "Food for People, Not for Profit."

Even a food cooperative needs to pay staff, vendors, buy products and make enough money to stay in business. It was no surprise that the co-op was bankrupt.

And then there was the staff. Every day was a new adventure. Some of the employees really tested Will's leadership. They didn't know him, he didn't know them. Some of the cashiers were very unprofessional.

There was one who, when he didn't like a customer, would throw their merchandise across the store. Will didn't think this was right. Some of the other cashiers would be sitting on the checkstand bagging area, leaning over to ring up customers. It was very unprofessional. Many also gave each other massages while ringing up customers.

Will's first termination was a cashier who refused to stop sitting in the bagging area. She said, "I'm going to sit here, that's what I've done and I'm going to continue to sit here." Will said, "Well you can go to the office now, I'm terminating you." This was his first termination.

He had to terminate a number of staff for outright insubordination. Most of them had never worked in a professional business before. Will wasn't happy about this, but he had to turn the business around quickly. After about a year, Will had cleaned house and brought more professional skilled staff on board.

Within a few months, Will had gotten rid of all the cashiers except me. Some of the terminations were ugly and the police were called for one of them. Another employee threatened to shoot Will and was fired soon after. He eventually found out that, until he arrived, no one had ever been fired before since the co-op started.

He knew he had to build a team of strong, talented managers and staff. Will didn't think anyone had a clue. But there was one person he noticed, Paul Bauersfeld, the grocery manager. Will found out Paul had a degree in economics. Will asked Paul the million dollar question, "Do you know what markup and margin is?" Paul said, "Of course…" Will had Paul give him an example. Will said to himself, "Holy mackerel! I found someone!" So now he had one person who could help row the bankrupt boat safely back to shore. Will made Paul his "second banana." (Actually his Store Manager, but this is a story about organic foods….)

Will and Paul got down to business. They started pricing things correctly, using traditional retail markups for each product department and category. Within a few months everything in the store was priced correctly, so sales would generate enough gross profit to cover expenses. Finally there was enough margin and profit from sales to build cash for the business.

Two key actions helped tremendously. Creating a sense of abundance—stocking enough product and in the right places—and marking up product correctly to create gross profit.

NO DOLLARS, NO SENSE

A new general manager or CEO of a business relies on financial information to effectively run the business. The Co-opportunity Will stepped into had no real numbers to review at that point. The last CPA the co-op used hadn't been paid. He wouldn't give back the books. Will was in the forest without a flashlight. The only financial records he had were on a yellow legal pad that the office manager used to scribble numbers on. Co-opportunity had been in Chapter 11 Bankruptcy since 1984. Nothing had been done to rectify the situation. Will didn't know how the store was able to stay open and operate as a business. The deadline from the government had long passed.

He had no idea how much money the co-op had in the bank at the time. It could've been five dollars, five hundred, five thousand or five hundred thousand, but it was probably closer to less than two thousand. Will contacted the bankruptcy attorney that had originally started the process to get Co-opportunity out of Chapter 11. Since nothing had been done in a while, the attorney couldn't find the file at first. So Will and the attorney began working on a plan to get Co-opportunity out of bankruptcy.

First, he had to get the financials, which were being held hostage by the co-op's accountant. It wasn't easy to get them back, since the co-op owed the accountant money, but Will eventually did. The financial picture he saw was not pretty. No taxes had been filed for the previous three years; the store had shown deep losses in previous years; the three most current month's financials were missing and the store hadn't once turned a profit since it opened in 1974.

"Well, I'll only be here three months…."

Will then contacted the state and worked on the process of getting Co-opportunity out of Chapter 11. He decided the best strategy was to hire a prestigious attorney to give the co-op more credibility. He found a new accountant in Beverly Hills who was willing to work with him. Will and the accountant managed to generate two years of financials and back taxes. This held the government at bay while Co-opportunity worked to pull itself out of the Chapter 11 ditch.

Will had to figure out who the co-op owed money to and how much. The coop had to repay debts to members, vendors and even staff. He worked from home and finally got it done. He issued letters to companies to which the co-op owed money and negotiated a plan to pay ten cents on every dollar owed. By the time the co-op was able to pay the money back (1988), the business was doing so well that the co-op actually paid sixty cents on every dollar owed. This was at the time the highest amount repaid by a company getting out of bankruptcy.

It took two years to get a repayment plan approved by the state. From 1988 to 1990 all the debt had been paid off and Co-opportunity was officially out of Chapter 11. After twelve years of losses, the co-op began to be profitable and generate cash from operations.

Sometime during the first few months he was there, Will also got a call from the U.S. Department of Agriculture (USDA). He was told they weren't going to renew Co-opportunity's license to sell fresh produce. Since the co-op was in bankruptcy, money was owed to many vendors, including interstate produce vendors. The USDA wanted a $50,000 cash bond from Co-opportunity. This would be held as a deposit to ensure that produce vendors would be paid. Will had two weeks to respond. He was able to negotiate smaller monthly payments of $5,000 a month for 10 months. The USDA would put this deposit on hold until two and half years after the co-op was out of bankruptcy. Will really didn't know where he would get the money to pay the deposit. But, as the co-op became more successful, the money became available. After we were completely cleared of Chapter 11 Bankruptcy in 1990, the USDA released the $50,000 deposit. Will remembers him and long-time board member, Michelle Jacobson, going together to the bank for the check. He said Michelle was singing all the way there….

The co-op board also grew in strength as the years went on. In the late 1980s, board members, David Schack, Michelle Jacobson and Carl

Fredlin formed a committee to completely revise and tighten up the bylaws. This also helped create a stronger organizational foundation for the co-op.

Once Will began making changes, sales and financial performance immediately improved. Sales jumped from under $900,000 before he started, to 1.2 million his first full year, then to 1.7 million, growing incrementally each year. The co-op also posted its first profitable year and remained profitable for many more years afterward.

WE WILL BUILD YOU A NEW STORE

By the early 1990s, the store was doing very well. At its most successful point, in 1994—the year before our current location opened—Co-opportunity was doing roughly 7 million dollars a year in sales in less than 3,000 sq. ft. of retail, with only 14 parking spaces. The store was jam-packed with members and shoppers, and was becoming almost impossible to deal with at that point. Remember, less than 10 years earlier, the store was bankrupt and about to close.

There was an empty lot across the street from the old store. Will met with the current landlord and asked him if he'd consider buying the lot and building us a new store. The landlord said no.

Then, one day, as Will was standing on the corner of 16th Street and Broadway, in front of the old store, an East Indian man walked up to him. He said he and his brothers had just bought the lot and they wanted to build a store for Co-opportunity. Will said his heart started fluttering. He contacted the board and soon after long-time board member Steve Bornstein, Will and another board member began negotiations for the new store. After about four months, negotiations became stalled over some disagreement between the two parties, so the board president stopped negotiations.

But Steve Bornstein was persistent. He decided to resume negotiations on his own with the property owners. Will had to convince the full board that doing nothing was more risky than the risk of an expansion. The process was resumed and soon after a lease and agreement were signed.

The new landlord would build the store for us, but it was up to Co-opportunity to fill the new building with equipment, fixtures (shelving, etc.) and product. There was one problem, while the co-op was financially strong and sales were growing, we still needed a large amount of cash to fund the expansion. We were only less than five years out of bankruptcy and didn't have enough cash in the bank for the project. Will tried to borrow from several banks, but with no luck. He finally contacted a financing company that agreed to loan us $250,000 based on our thriving condition at the time.

1525 BROADWAY

The new store would be a big improvement over the existing store. It was located directly across the street at 1525 Broadway. The parking lot had 41 spaces. This was a huge increase over the old store. Will didn't even think we needed that many. The store was over 9,000 sq. ft. which was much larger than the old store's 3,000 sq. ft.

So Co-opportunity was moving to a new home. With only $250,000 to spend, tough decisions had to be made. Will wanted the store to look great, so most of the $250,000 was budgeted for equipment, fixtures, store design, etc. We still needed to fill the store with a lot more inventory than in the old store. And we were adding a huge amount of new items. Will and his key product managers negotiated with all of our vendors. They told them if they wanted their product on our shelves, they'd have to fill our new store with free product. The strategy worked so well that every company we dealt with gave us two free cases of every product in the store. Since the new store was much larger, we expanded item selection in every department - especially in the vitamin and cosmetic departments.

Will wanted something special in the front of the store to celebrate our grand opening. So he installed an electric waterfall with a rock façade, colored lights, trees, and foliage right at the store entrance where customers entered. Eventually, this would be replaced with actual product for sale, but the waterfall definitely made an impression. Also, a local artist, Valerie Sharp, was hired to paint a mural all around the store's interior walls above the shelving and equipment.

Will also creatively marketed the upcoming grand opening in the local paper. The ad showed a winding road in black and white, with one stone colored yellow. Each week, as the grand opening got closer, another part of the road would be colored yellow. The yellow brick road got larger and larger until grand opening week. The final ad showed a winding yellow brick road leading to a picture of the new store.

The few weeks before opening, Will said he couldn't even sleep. He was very worried the store wouldn't meet sales projections. We opened on a Saturday in December of 1994. Within 30 minutes of opening, the parking lot was full. Once Will saw this, he knew the new store would be a success. People loved the new store. We got praise from everyone. For the first three days, Will stood by the door and handed out flowers to everyone who came in. Women loved them. Most of the men declined.

We had been doing close to 7 million dollars in sales in the old store. Projections for the new store's first year were a conservative 8 million. The first year actually saw sales of over 10 million.

While the move was risky, the competitive landscape had changed a lot in the twenty years since Co-opportunity first began. More natural foods chains were sprouting up, and the food our co-op sold was not as alien to the mainstream shopper. We were once the niche market, catering to health-conscious people who wanted the purest organic products available - most not sold in mainstream markets. Now that more people were aware of the effects of food on health, more and more consumers wanted "natural, organic and fresh" food. It was important that our co-op have enough space to provide a wider range of products and services such as a fresh deli, so we could continue growing, even with increased competition.

The new Co-opportunity on 1525 Broadway grew from 10 million in sales in 1995, to over 14 million in 2005, when Will retired. We weathered increased competition, especially from Whole Foods and

Wild Oats. We grew our membership base tremendously, eventually signing up roughly 100 new members a month.

Will focused on creating a fun, humor-filled, positive store environment, for both shoppers and employees. He focused on paying staff well and providing good benefits to increase staff retention and satisfaction. He also strategically built up cash reserves so when competition arrived, if our sales went down temporarily, we could "weather the storm" until sales eventually bounced back - which they always did.

A few years before Will retired, the board began a hiring process to search for a new general manager. I applied for the position and eventually got the job. After working for 20 years under Will's leadership, I was now in charge. The store was in a similar position as the old store was in 1994, before we moved. It was thriving and needed more space. Sales per square foot in 2006 were so high that one of the consultants hired to help determine growth options said we were "abusing our customers," since our store was now supposedly too small to handle the sales volume.

When Will retired in 2006, Co-opportunity had 1.8 million in cash in the bank. Twenty years before, we were in bankruptcy and had virtually nothing. Will left Co-opportunity in a financially solid position, debt-free, and poised to thrive and grow even more. It was now up to myself, our board and our talented staff to help lead our little community-grown co-op forward into the future.

OUR LITTLE CO-OP THAT COULD
2006 – PRESENT AND BEYOND
BY BRUCE PALMA, GENERAL MANAGER

After working under Will Simon's leadership for 20 years, I became the new general manager in 2006. I had applied for the position in 2005, and after an extensive hiring process conducted by our board, I was chosen. Since I had worked in the store for so long, I had a fairly clear internal perspective on operations, staff and customer culture—and a whole big list of things I wanted to change. While

Will had worked miracles in the early years, and also turned our new location into a great success, more changes were needed for our co-op to continue growing and thriving for another 20 – 30 years. But there was a big difference: our co-op in 2006 was in vastly better shape than the one Will inherited in 1985. We had cash in the bank, strong sales, and consultants saying we needed to expand, and consumer interest in natural and organic foods was growing. My job, with the invaluable help of our managers and staff, was to hunker down and make key changes to create positive results. The car ran well; the engine was solid; we were ready for a longer journey. We just needed a tune up and an oil change.

Since I had worked many positions during Will's time, including, cashier supervisor, manager-on-duty, HR manager, operations and store manager, I was ready to jump in and make changes everywhere. I had also met with all of our employees a few months before the job started. My HR manager and I held brainstorming meetings with small groups of staff. We wanted to get direct input, feedback and ideas from the staff to inform my plans moving forward. This was invaluable. It helped me create a plan to show the board and managers how our co-op could continue to grow and improve. I also worked hard to create an effective management team.

Once I started, the changes came fast and furious. We made improvements to labor costs, profit margins, customer service, merchandising, inventory control and many other areas. In many ways, we did exactly what Will did, only within a new context. We figured out what shoppers wanted, merchandised and priced it right, tightened up our customer service, controlled costs and improved the shopping environment.

The key idea was that change was good, and absolutely necessary if a business is to not only survive, but continue to grow and thrive.

It wasn't easy. I had to make some tough decisions, with staff accountability and operations. While some of the staff didn't immediately like all the changes, in the end, most saw the benefit. We improved productivity, controlled labor costs and increased our sales and gross margin almost immediately. We were able to increase staff benefits and pay as well. I became GM in January, 2006—half way through our fiscal year. At that point, we were $60,000 in the "red" – we were showing a loss with only six months to turn it around. We ended that fiscal year with over a 10% sales increase and a healthy profit.

We continued to grow for a few years until the recession in 2008 – 2009. During that fiscal year, at its worst point, our sales were negative 7% after several years of double-digit growth. After creating a monthly one-day, 10% member sale day, our sales bounced back enough to help us end our fiscal year with flat sales—no sales growth but, more importantly, no sales loss. Flat was better than negative. We were also profitable. Here's the best part: we didn't have to cut any staff hours or lay off any staff.

After bouncing back from the recession, it was clear something needed to be done with our facility. Our lease was ending in a few years, and we either needed to find a larger, more suitable location or lock in a new lease term for our current site. We had spent several years searching for a new and larger location, but found nothing. We had a very successful lease re-negotiation with our landlord, locking in a 20-year term with no huge increase in rent. We had always had a good relationship with our landlord, and both parties were happy to continue working together.

I had also contacted Sutti and Associates, a grocery store remodeling and development company, to assess our current site and its future growth potential. John Sutti, one of the company's principals, said our location had more potential, and that we had built up a lot of goodwill and recognition there. We just needed to give our shoppers more of what they wanted and were already getting somewhere else. Sutti had extensive experience with store development and remodels. They had worked with other co-ops, Whole Foods and many other independent grocers.

We decided to give our store, once new and exciting in 1995, a complete makeover in 2011. The remodel was done over seven months while the store was open. Most of the work was done at night when the store was closed. The entire store was changed. The transition was so successful, we only lost 2% of sales during the remodel. Our members and shoppers were very forgiving. Each day they came in, something was changed. One day the produce section was in one place, the next day it had been moved. This was the same for all departments. We replaced all the equipment and fixtures in the entire store, added a new floor, lighting and other improvements.

Once done, our store was a completely different place. We expanded our food service operations, adding a salad bar, hot food bar and expanded service deli. We had a new demo counter and cheese section. We increased product selections in all departments and gave the store a complete makeover. Sutti had projected a 17% sales increase after the remodel, and, thanks to Sutti and the hard work of all our staff, we had a 16.5% increase. We somehow managed to squeeze more juice out of the lemon—even though the consultants had told us we were at capacity many years before.

WHERE DO WE GO FROM HERE?

So here we are. It's 2015. Our co-op just celebrated its 41st year in business. From four founding members to over 10,000 active members and 115 employees; from less than $100,000 a year in sales to over 24 million in sales; once a tiny cramped storefront on Santa Monica Boulevard, now a bustling community hub with over 2,000 customers a day.

But we're not alone. We're linked as a "virtual chain" with over 125 sister co-ops nationwide through our membership in the National Co+op Grocers (NCG). The NCG exemplifies the true spirit of one of the seven cooperative principles, "Cooperation among Cooperatives." The principle embodies our own co-op's mission and vision, and also that of the NCG:

Cooperatives serve their members most effectively and strengthen the cooperative movement by working together through local, national, regional and international structures.

Our membership in the NCG over the past decade has helped our co-op immensely. Through our combined buying power, we've secured competitive wholesale product costs; have access to the combined wisdom of hundreds of other retail food co-ops, professional development, peer support, training and operational resources and much more. Most importantly, we're helping each other sustain and grow our businesses and remain competitive in an industry with fierce competition. We're actively working on expanding to multiple locations, so we can expose even more people to our co-operative experience and provide an alternative to the corporate chain grocers.

In the end, we don't know exactly what our future holds; but it's our goal that Co-opportunity continue to creatively grow—not only as a business, but also as a community of people sharing in the co-operative experience, further enhancing the quality of life for our staff, members and shoppers, strengthening our local economy and helping create a more peaceful, sustainable planet.

Having gone from four founders to over 10,000 members and growing our future potential is truly unlimited. Many of our sister co-ops are growing by expanding their existing stores, moving to larger stores nearby or developing additional stores in the area. Fortunately, we can learn which strategy works best and grow ourselves to serve more members in our community. A new future awaits us.

"Throughout the history of these 1970s co-ops an important additional benefit they have provided is active learning and experience using the cooperative structure for further enterprises. Today, there is even greater potential for co-ops, and a crying need for more of Co-opportunity's kind democratically-owned structure and community-based services. **"**

Dave Gutknecht, Editor, Cooperative Grocer

CHAPTER 17
120 MORE FOOD CO-OPS ARE ON THE WAY
by Stuart Reid of FCI

WHAT NEWLY FORMING CO-OPS CAN LEARN FROM CO-OPPORTUNITY

Starting a new co-op is a labor of love—it always was and always will be. Why else would a group of people with no grocery experience volunteer thousands of hours to open a new business? A business with a return on investment that Wall Street would scoff at? Because a food co-op provides its owners, workers, shoppers, and community with far more than financial speculation. Not only the obvious benefits of better food, better jobs, better support for the local economy, but also the expanding impact of cooperation can catalyze the revitalization of entire neighborhoods. Co-ops may or may not pay out cash dividends, but they always provide an amazing return in social capital.

David Thompson's loving history of Co-opportunity reflects the often messy, sometimes frustrating, and always rewarding process of starting and nurturing, a new food co-op. Every one of the beautiful and vibrant co-ops we enjoy today (and often take for granted) started with the hard work, commitment and dreams of a small group of people. Their efforts inspire a new generation of co-op organizers as a "third wave" of food co-ops washes across the U.S.

Over the last ten years, hundreds of communities have recognized the need for a cooperative alternative to mainstream grocery options. Already over 70 new co-ops have opened in rural villages, urban centers, college towns, suburbs, and even in areas like Minneapolis/ St Paul, Minnesota, where successful food co-ops already dot the landscape. New co-ops have opened from Sierra Vista, on the Mexican border, to Fairbanks, Alaska, near the Arctic Circle; from Mandela Foods Cooperative in Oakland, California, to Monadnock Co-op in Keene, New Hampshire.

There are over 120 more that are organizing right now. Why the renewed interest? I believe it is in large part due to the impact that "New Wave" co-ops like Co-opportunity have had on the people who experience the power of cooperation first-hand. In our mobile society, families often relocate and when they leave a co-op behind, its absence leaves an empty space in their lives that inspires them to start a food co-op in their new community.

Following the Cooperative Principle of cooperation among cooperatives, co-ops like Co-opportunity have provided invaluable guidance and support for these newcomers, with mentoring, staff training, and even financial assistance. Financial support from the co-op community has also enabled the creation of Food Co-op Initiative, a non-profit organization dedicated entirely to enabling more successful new food co-ops. Through Food Co-op Initiative and other co-op development organizations, food co-op founders have access to tools, resources and guidance based on the successes and experience of the entire food co-op community. All of this help is critical to the new wave of co-ops. While the founders of Co-opportunity had to blaze their own trails, learning as they went, lobbying for legislative change, and creating the structures they needed to flourish, new co-ops today are the beneficiaries of that dedicated effort, gaining a huge head start—and they need it.

In the 70s and 80s, there was no natural food industry and very few grocery stores paid any attention to "health food." Today, competition is intense and growing. Co-ops don't have the luxury of a captive market. They must meet the challenge of competitors using sophisticated marketing, low-cost prices enabled by immense buying power, and even internet-based convenience.

Instead of starting a co-op with 20 members and a $5,000 in capital like Co-opportunity in 1975, new co-ops are opening with 800-1,000 member - or more. Startup budgets have risen to $1-3 Million - or more. More than half of that capital has to come from owner-members and their community. How is it even possible that co-ops can build that kind of support? Once again, we must thank the pioneers who came before us for showing the world that co-ops pay returns beyond what can be measured in dollars. Communities—individuals, families, farmers, civic organizations, local government—are willing to invest in that which they believe. We cannot start a co-op using the business strategies of the previous wave, but we can and must emulate their unwavering determination.

Those of us supporting new co-op development owe a debt of gratitude for everything co-ops like Co-opportunity have done to pave the way. The idealism, commitment, and tireless effort of their founders and members continue to inspire us. Thanks to David Thompson, storyteller and historian, for reminding us of our roots and honoring the people whose vision leads to our cooperative future.

"Congratulations to the Co-opportunity Members. Whether you knew it or not, you were pioneers in transforming the US food industry!**"**

Karen Zimbelman, Director of Membership and Cooperative Relations, National Co+op™ Grocers

CHAPTER 18
ACCOLADES FROM CO-OP LEADERS ACROSS AMERICA

In his history of Co-opportunity, David Thompson has written the founding tale of cooperatives throughout the world. It tells of visionary people with a dream to help save the world, with little capital, a lot of perseverance and a roadmap called the Cooperative Principles. The story has been re-enacted countless times and has resulted in the creation of numerous organizations pursuing a form of commerce that truly does account for the greater good.

But this is also a story about Co-opportunity as it celebrates 40 years of service to its community, and of the dedicated cooperators who have made it, and continue to make it, a vibrant asset for making Santa Monica a better place to live. This book contains a long list of contributors to the beginnings and eventual success of Co-opportunity. For many of its formative years, David Thompson played a leading role. He writes from the perspective of one who believed (and helped shape) the vision, and then did all he could to make it a reality, attending meetings, making contacts, speaking out on issues and in living the dream. He also writes with obvious affection for his co-conspirators and for the numerous California cooperative ventures they sustained.

David Thompson is a vital resource in chronicling the history of the cooperative movement. He has written a book that should be read by the next wave of cooperators who now follow in the footsteps of the Co-opportunity founders. It is a book that can inspire their work.

Terry Appleby, General Manager, Hanover Consumer Cooperative Society, Chair, National Co+op™ Grocers Board of Directors (2014)

This book is a tribute to the spirit of cooperation in Santa Monica, California, and to Co-opportunity in their beginning years. The personal testimony of author David Thompson shines a light on all the ways the co-op has made a major difference in their community, as well as demonstrating how the heady days of 1960s and 1970s activism influenced food co-op development.

In this narrative, Thompson also makes important connections between "old wave" cooperatives and the ascendance of the "new wave"—something that has been little explored in food co-op chronicles. Additionally, Thompson pays homage to Toyohiko Kagawa, the deeply influential Japanese cooperator who was considered co-father of many California cooperatives. Yet no history of cooperatives is only about key players. Above all, scores of people had a profound desire to change the way people participate in the economy, one that is people-first, based on fairness, and community-focused. Co-opportunity and its history is an embodiment of how the common good has been served in Santa Monica and beyond.

In "Co-opportunity: The Rise of a Community Owned Market," Thompson describes himself and others as earnest and committed, people who didn't set out to make history, but their determination to contribute has left a unique legacy. These are important, poignant, well-written stories that contribute to a powerful understanding of the motivations and accomplishments of the American food co-op movement.

Patricia Cumbie, author of "Growing with Purpose, Forty Years of Seward Community Cooperative"

Co-opportunity demonstrates the positive community impacts and enduring legacy of cooperative democracy. It has already been 25 years since "Co-opportunity Comeback" was published on the cover of food co-ops' trade magazine, Cooperative Grocer. Going back even further, as David Thompson reminds us, Co-opportunity had renewed the consumer co-op tradition formerly embodied in the Santa Monica Co-op and Associated Cooperatives.

Around the country, more than a hundred such food co-ops survived their experimental, often shaky operations of the 1970s – and all those co-ops benefited in important ways from our cooperative predecessors. Together, co-op member-owners have the opportunity and obligation to share and pass on this cooperative legacy and wealth-building.

The history of Co-opportunity and its many sister food co-ops around the country, despite the many setbacks, is a proud and influential one. These cooperatives have been critical in supporting and expanding the organic farming sector, which was tiny at first but has become the fastest-growing part of our food system. Co-opportunity and co-ops across the country pioneered in offering cleaner food and still lead their communities in education about our food supply. They do this while modeling democracy in action through cooperative enterprise: providing high-quality goods and expanding services, modeling transparent policies and governance, and keeping more capital in the local community while facilitating broader ownership.

Throughout the history of these 1970s co-ops an important additional benefit they have provided is active learning and experience using the cooperative structure for further enterprises. Today, there is even greater potential for co-ops, and a crying need for more of Co-opportunity's kind democratically-owned structure and community-based services.

Dave Gutknecht, Editor, Cooperative Grocer

Filled with unforgettable characters and atmospheric details, Thompson's Co-opportunity chronicle tells an inspiring tale of community dedication to a common goal. Though set in California, the events have been repeated in scores of communities since the early 1970s. Coming out of the civil rights and anti-war activism of the 1960s, people throughout the country have learned that working together they could make significant and lasting change. Thompson's rich story makes you want to join a co-op just to hang out with these remarkable people who support community-owned businesses.

From countless meetings in a Santa Monica garage to a $25 million community owned business, the story of Co-opportunity, its roots in the Santa Monica Co-op and its local and national impact is an inspiration to communities everywhere. The tale is a community activist's must-read about committed and engaging characters who prevail over legal and financial obstacles and personality and political conflicts.

Thompson's deep knowledge of co-operative history; his vast personal experience; and his insights on community organizing add enormously to this absorbing history of Co-opportunity. This is a well-told story about successful and constructive community collaboration in a heady time of social change. It offers cooperatives as a significant, realistic and people-centered option for communities recovering from the Great Recession.

Ann Hoyt, Cooperative Hall of Fame Inductee 2015, former Chair, National Cooperative Business Association, CCMA Superstar

---

David Thompson was my next-door neighbor on Princeton Street in Santa Monica during the period covered by this book. Tina Handy and Michael Hyatt, who both worked at Co-opportunity, also lived in our fourplex. In fact, David wouldn't let the landlord rent to anyone who didn't work at or support the co-op.

During that time, David gave every spare hour to birthing, nurturing and boosting Co-opportunity. David committed the kind of mental and physical energy that only a "true believer" possesses.

His work on LA's Westside and Santa Monica created a sustainable foundation that put Co-opportunity on the map and allowed it to grow and to prosper. Co-opportunity also provided a roadmap for others who wanted to emulate this success in their own communities.

Years later, when I was elected from the San Fernando Valley to the California State Assembly, David was often in my office advocating for better laws for consumer and housing cooperatives.

It was easy to be a sponsor of David's efforts on co-op legislation regarding capital, cooperative housing and the California Center for Cooperatives.

It was easy because David always brings the highest degree of integrity to whatever he is working on. He never sought the "fame or fortune" that blinds so many others. He has never lost sight of the reasons for doing what he did - to empower others; to show folks how to have a greater say in their own lives, in their own choices and to bring out the best in people.

To many in the California Legislature, David is "Mr. Co-op." To me, he's all that and more. But most importantly David is one of my longest and dearest friends.

Richard Katz, former California Assembly Democratic Leader, California Assembly Member (1980-1996)

For over 30 years, David Thompson has been my eyes and ears to the world of cooperatives. His account of Co-opportunity's beginnings and achievements reinforces my appreciation of the contribution of coops in the area of my greatest passions, from democratic governance to ecological farming and food. Thanks, Co-opportunity, for your contribution to a better world. Happy 40th Anniversary.

Frances Moore Lappé, Co-Founder Small Planet Institute and author of 18 books including "Diet for a Small Planet" and "EcoMind "

Thank you, David, for documenting the history of Co-oportunity and their 40 years of service. And congratulations to Bruce and the Board on reaching this impressive milestone. From all of us at North Coast Co-op, a hearty welcome to the 40 year club!

David Lippman, Former General Manager, North Coast Cooperative & Board Member, Twin Pines Cooperative Foundation

Cooperators will be fascinated by how strongly this part history lesson, part memoir resonates with our own co-op stories, and appreciate that someone has taken the time to chronicle our shared experience in such detail and personal witness.

David Thompson's life is a Forest Gump-like journey through the co-op world. This book weaves through not only the story of Co-opportunity, but the food co-op and co-op movement in general. It's a treasure.

Dan Nordley, Publisher, Cooperative Grocer and Past Director, Cooperative Grocer Information Network

---

For decades, and in communities across the country, retail food co-ops like Co-opportunity have been leaders in providing consumers with high-quality local, organic and sustainably produced food. Born out of the ideas and philosophies of the 1960s counterculture, these "new wave" co-ops were the pioneers of today's natural foods industry; providing markets for natural, organically grown and fairly traded products, introducing bulk foods, and increasing awareness of the importance of eating fresh, whole foods.

Once the only place to find natural and organic foods, co-ops today compete in increasingly competitive markets that challenge our relevance. Successful co-ops like Co-opportunity, now celebrating their 40th anniversary, know that sound business practices are as essential to success as are a commitment to people and environment, and that strong membership support, sufficient capital, ability to adapt to changes in the marketplace, and an openness to finding more ways to work together are all critical to our success -- as individual co-ops and as a united cooperative sector.

Co-ops like Co-opportunity have built resilient and vibrant businesses, and their successful practices and accumulated knowledge need to be leveraged! Together, we can realize our vision of more co-ops, benefiting more people, in more communities. We are stronger together!

Robynn Shrader, CEO, National Co+op™ Grocers

Congratulations to the Co-opportunity Members

Whether you knew it or not, you were pioneers in transforming the US food industry!

Co-opportunity is part of a small group of pioneering food co-ops that were on the forefront of every positive recent reform in the food industry. Our predecessor co-ops, many of whom were started in the 1930s and 40s, are still leading the way with consumer reforms that required nutritional labeling and unit pricing on store shelves (to better compare prices).

Then, in the late 1960s and 70s, the "new wave" of consumer co-ops began. Like its peers, Co-opportunity was born out of the ideas and philosophies of the 1960s, with a deep passion for equality, social justice, and to making whole foods available to its members. This set off a quiet revolution in what eventually became the "natural foods" industry.

Co-opportunity has been a leader in Santa Monica, by providing great food and shared ownership of the store to its thousands of member-owners. The co-op has also provided leadership to the strong and powerful network of food co-ops around the U.S., a group that uses its collective buying power and economic muscle to continue to be a positive change agent in all steps from farm to fork.

Co-opportunity, like its peers and many co-ops to come, has learned to leverage its cooperative ownership structure to bring economic power to the people. The impact has been enormous – both in its local community, as well as throughout the country. Here's to many more years of consumer empowerment and continued growth of a strong and vibrant cooperative sector – in Santa Monica and beyond.

Karen Zimbelman, Director of Membership and Cooperative Relations, National Co+op™ Grocers

"In 2015, the Twin Pines Cooperative Foundation also celebrates 50 years as the longest serving foundation for consumer cooperatives in the United States. Stephanie Mandel said that the BriarPatch Co-op is a direct beneficiary of the foundation's long-term vision. "It was the determination of people 50 years ago that we are benefiting from today. You should know that your efforts today to establish a Cooperative Community Fund through the Twin Pines Cooperative Foundation matter.**"**

Stephanie Mandel, Marketing Manager, Briarpatch Co-op, Grass Valley, CA

CHAPTER 19
LET'S WIN THE $10,000 MATCHING GRANT!

$10,000 CHALLENGE GRANT FOR OUR CO-OPPORTUNITY COOPERATIVE COMMUNITY FUND

Both the people who created and those who have supported Co-opportunity on its path have dreams of building a better world. You can help us build a road to that future by matching the $10,000 grant being offered ($5,000 by the board of Co-opportunity and an additional $5,000 match by Co-opportunity Co-Founder, David J. Thompson). Every dollar (up to $10,000) contributed to the Co-opportunity Cooperative Community Fund by December 31st, 2017, will be matched on a one-to-one basis. A $20,000 infusion will boost the CCCF to about $70,000.

All proceeds from the sale of this book will also be donated to the CCCF.

By 2015, the Cooperative Community Fund program will be sponsored by about 40 partner food co-ops across the country. Joined together under the umbrella of the Twin Pines Cooperative Foundation (TPCF), TPCF and the CCFs donate over $100,000 per year to local nonprofits in the 40 communities served by our sponsor food co-ops.

TPCF and the CCF program are the largest single co-op investors in cooperative development organizations (CDOs) in the United States. Food Co-ops around the country like Co-opportunity get most of their early funding from those CDOs. The almost $3 million of TPCF and CCF assets leverages nearly $30 million dollars in conventional capital for the development of US food cooperatives.

TPCF and the CCF program are also the largest single co-op investors in Equal Exchange, Maple Valley and Organic Valley. Our funds boost Fair Trade and the organic dairy and maple syrup cooperatives.

By donating to your CCCF you are doubling your donation, you are increasing by 50% the ability of the CCCF to donate to local nonprofits and you are immediately creating another $200,000 of funds towards the development of US food cooperatives. Every dollar you donate makes the food co-op family stronger in so many ways.

You can see the results of our shared work at www.community.coop.

During the Golden Jubilee of the Twin Pines Cooperative Foundation, the CCF program will make a matching grant of $5,000 each to eleven new food co-ops to start a CCF. This $75,000 in matches has been contributed by the Blooming Prairie Foundation, Cabot Creamery, Capital Impact, Equal Exchange, Frontier Co-op, National Cooperative Bank, National Cooperative Grocers, Organic Valley and The Cooperative Foundation. With $110,000 from eleven more food co-ops, the CDOs will have another million dollars to leverage during TPCF's Golden Jubilee Year (2015).

GIVE WHERE YOU LIVE - THANKS!

GIVE WHERE YOU LIVE
IMPACT OF A COOPERATIVE COMMUNITY FUND
BY PATRICIA CUMBIE

When cooperatives work together to set aside funds to benefit groups in their local communities, the impact is exponential. That's what food cooperatives have discovered when they establish their own Cooperative Community Fund (CCF) through the Twin Pines Cooperative Foundation's (TPCF) Give Where You Live Campaign. The funds typically start with a food co-op investing $5,000 and their investment is matched by the foundation or their cooperative partners. Currently, over forty food co-ops in the U.S. have established their own CCF.

2015 is the Golden Jubilee of the Twin Pines Cooperative Foundation and twenty more co-ops have applied to join our CCF program.

One of those cooperative partners is Organic Valley, a farmer-owned co-op located in LaFarge, Wisconsin. They've made $30,000 in matching grants to Twin Pines for food co-ops wishing to create their own community funds. "This is cooperation among co-ops," said Jerry McGeorge, vice president of cooperative affairs at Organic Valley, of the program. "We have a rich history ourselves of trying to be responsible community members. We saw this as an opportunity to extend our reach and help other co-ops fulfill something important to them in their communities," he said.

With an initial start of $10,000, those food co-ops have the opportunity to build their fund and the capacity to donate the interest earned to local community groups. It's a win-win-win for cultivating co-op capital, bringing people together for communal fundraising events, and for serving the needs of a wide range of people.

The Hanover Consumer Co-op in Hanover, New Hampshire, established their fund in 2001 with a matching grant, and currently their endowment is almost $400,000. Their goal is to grow to it to $1 million dollars so that the annual interest earned for distribution is even more impactful. "The Hanover Cooperative Community Fund does double-duty," said Terry Appleby, the co-op's general manager. "It helps co-ops and it allows us to give a portion back to our community." The HCCF is grown and sustained through a number of cooperative events, including a walk-a-thon, golf tournament, proceeds from a wine sale and during Co-op Month in October all of the earnings from their Community Partners Program goes to the HCCF.

On the West coast, the BriarPatch Co-op Community Market in Grass Valley, California has seen their CCF grow to over $100,000 in the decade since they started it. Their fundraising activities have included anything from raffles, bring-a-bag donations, silent auctions, staging benefit concerts, asking co-op members to donate their patronage dividends, and partnering with fair trade distributor Equal Exchange to donate 2% of specified product sales to their co-op community fund. Their fund has supported 45 organizations in their community that are working to protect the environment, create farm to school programs, offer social services and food assistance, garden projects, English as a second language, and many others. There is virtually no part of their community that has not been assisted by their fund.

Stephanie Mandel, the marketing director at BriarPatch said, "People at our co-op feel good about it and like being part of something bigger than themselves by helping others through the fund." She said that all of the efforts big and small on behalf of the community fund have contributed to promoting a community spirit and caring for others. Mandel also noted that because of the way the community fund is structured, the money will keep doing good on into the future.

In 2015, the Twin Pines Cooperative Foundation also celebrates 50 years as the longest serving foundation for consumer cooperatives in the United States. Mandel said that BriarPatch is a direct beneficiary of the foundation's long-term vision. "It was the determination of people 50 years ago that we are benefiting from today. You should know that your efforts today to establish a cooperative community fund through Twin Pines matter," she said. Appleby concurred, "It's an inspiring organization."

HOW TO START A COOPERATIVE COMMUNITY FUND

The Twin Pines Cooperative Foundation is pleased to announce that their organization has received funding of $75,000 from the Blooming Prairie Foundation, Cabot Creamery, Capital Impact Partners, The Cooperative Foundation, Equal Exchange, Frontier Co-op, National Cooperative Bank, National Cooperative Grocers Association and Organic Valley to match funds from cooperatives that want to start their own Cooperative Community Fund. Come join us.

Contact David J. Thompson at 530-757-2233 or at dthompcoop@aol.com to get on the interest list. To find out more about the foundation the community fund go to www.community.coop/ccf.

Patricia Cumbie is a writer and co-op education consultant living in Minneapolis. She enjoys ownership in a wide variety of co-ops and has devoted her career to the cooperative movement.

BEST WISHES TO CO-OPPORTUNITY
ON YOUR FIRST FORTY YEARS AND FOR THE NEXT FORTY YEARS

**From all of us at the
Twin Pines Cooperative Foundation**

**We're happy to have contributed $10,000
of our funds in the early 2000's to kick off your
Co-opportunity Cooperative Community Fund**

**We look forward to working with you to boost your
Co-opportunity Cooperative Community Fund
to $100,000**

In 2015 we add another $500 to the matching funds

- By the end of 2016 there will be about 60 US food co-ops operating a Cooperative Community Fund (CCF) program.

- TPCF/CCF's $3 million of investment in cooperative development organizations leverages $30 million in funds for the development of US food co-ops.

The Twin Pines Cooperative Foundation is pleased to announce that in 2015 they have received funding of $75,000 from the Blooming Prairie Foundation, Cabot Creamery, Capital Impact Partners, The Cooperative Foundation, Equal Exchange, Frontier Co-op, National Cooperative Bank, National Co+op Grocers and Organic Valley to match funds from cooperatives that want to start their own Cooperative Community Fund.

We thank these co-ops for their support.

TWIN PINES COOPERATIVE FOUNDATION
WWW.COMMUNITY.COOP

MY BEST WISHES FOR THE FUTURE OF CO-OPPORTUNITY

Over forty years ago a small group of people started an idea which became over time the Co-opportunity we know today.

I am proud to know the past but more importantly I am invested in the future.

My hope is that the gift of $5,000 from Co-opportunity and $5,000 from me will be matched by the members of Co-opportunity to grow the present endowment of over $50,000 in the Co-opportunity Cooperative Community Fund.

With the help of the members and others this 41st Anniversary phase will push the CCCF past the $100,000 mark.

Every dollar is invested in the development of food co-ops and all the earnings are given back to nonprofits in the Santa Monica community.

As a result, you and I will know forever that Co-opportunity will have a tool for tomorrow for giving back to the community.

David J. Thompson,
Co-Founder Co-opportunity

CO-OP FUN FACTS

More Americans **own shares in credit unions and co-ops** than own shares on the New York, American and NASDAQ Stock Exchanges.

The **largest single mortgage in the world is Co-op City** in the Bronx Borough of New York City with 15,500 housing units on one mortgage.

Penn South, in New York City was the **first housing cooperative dedicated by a US president.** On May 19, 1962, President John F. Kennedy dedicated the 3,000 unit cooperative.

One of every three Americans is a member of a cooperative. There over 100 million members of cooperatives.

America's dairy co-ops market **80% of the nation's milk production.**

The only business which operates in the White House, the U. S. Capitol, the Pentagon and the United Nations is **a Credit Union.**

Rural electric co-ops provide electricity to 80% of America's land mass.

AUTHOR'S BIO

David J. Thompson immigrated to the United States from England in 1962, and moved to Southern California in 1965. He first lived in Los Angeles and then Santa Monica from 1966-1979. He attended Santa Monica College, where he won the Dean Ruenitz Award, and later UCLA, where he received a BA in Sociology and an MA at the School of Architecture and Urban Planning, along with receiving the Dean's Award for Community Service.

He was active in the anti-war movement, civil rights movement, as well as being a long-time volunteer for the United Farm Workers Union. David served on the security team during Robert Kennedy's presidential campaign in California and often on the security team for Cesar Chavez.

David became involved in the old Santa Monica Co-op in 1968. In 1973, he became one of the four founding members of Co-opportunity. David served on the Board of Co-opportunity until October of 1978. He represented Co-opportunity on the board of Associated Cooperatives from 1977-1980, and on the Board of the California Cooperative Foundation. David left Santa Monica in spring of 1979, to live in Sacramento and then soon thereafter Davis.

David co-chaired the California efforts to win passage of legislation establishing the National Cooperative Bank, working closely with Senator Alan Cranston and Senator Hayakawa to that end. David then went to Washington to become the first co-op employee of the Bank. He did everything required of him to help the Bank get started. The early political struggles over the existence of the Bank were numerous. David and a few others made sure the Bank made it through the many political hurdles erected to put the Bank out of business.

David became the first Western Regional Director for the National Cooperative Bank. Later, David was appointed Director of International Relations for the National Cooperative Business Association. He also co-chaired the efforts to establish the Center for Cooperatives at the University of California.

David moved to Davis permanently in 1980, where he served for 17 years as a board member of the Davis Food Co-op. He once again serves on the board of Associated Cooperatives, and is the President of the Twin Pines Cooperative Foundation (www.community.coop).

He is now a consultant to cooperatives in the areas of nonprofit, mutual and cooperative housing and cooperative development. He has written "Weavers of Dreams: Founders of the Modern Cooperative Movement," co-written "Cooperation Works" with E.G. Nadeau, contributed to 30 other books and written over 400 articles on cooperatives. David remains a full shareholder at Co-opportunity and visits the store about once every other year.

In 2010, David Thompson was inducted into the Cooperative Hall of Fame for his work on behalf of cooperatives, and, in particular, helping found Co-opportunity. You can see his induction and early photos of Co-opportunity in his induction video at http://community. coop/twinpines/hof/index.html